The medicine-making guide to native medicinal plants and their uses

THE NATIVE AMERICANS
Herbal Dispensatory

HANDBOOK

Learn the medicinal purposes and how to use homegrown herbal plants

Philip Kuckunniw

Copyright

Philip Kuckunniw
© Copyright 2020 - All rights reserved.

Disclaimer

Copyright

Philip Kuckunniw
© Copyright 2020 - All rights reserved.

Disclaimer

All intellect contained in this book is given for enlightening and instructive purposes as it were. The creator isn't in any capacity responsible for any outcomes or results that radiate from utilising this material. Worthwhile endeavours have been made to give data that is both precise and viable. However, the creator isn't oriented for the exactness or use/misuse of this data.

Table of Contents

Introduction

HERBALISM expands further than the historical backdrop of humanity. Everything that we realize today follows the strings from the earliest starting point, woven together into an embroidered artwork of information that we will, in general, underestimate. However, it is normal to search out plants for medication, as creatures do.

From the family hound eating grass for a harsh stomach to chimps picking restorative plants for explicit purposes (pain, parasites, and so on.), there is a decent arrangement of proof that creatures and people the same go-to plants for healing. We hold inborn information that is frequently overlooked and disregarded.

With the modernization of medication, town botanists were evaded. For instance, herbal healers in Pennsylvania-German district followed what is privately known as Pow-wow, or all the more appropriately, Braucherei. It is a blend of Native American healing, old German medication, and petition that a large number of the old-clocks around here recollect as a real existence sparing therapeutic strategy when customary medication fizzled.

During the 1950s, it was driven underground, as were most local healing customs around the globe, as customary medication was grasped. Just in the most recent decade have people started to chip away at saving and securing these conventions. Albeit some herbal healing modalities in nations, for example, India and China, have prospered, even there the country cultivators are right now working with individuals who are reporting their work and the herbs they use.

In the Amazonian rainforests, analysts are hustling to gain from the town cultivators before time runs out. This work is being completed far and wide as our older folks pass on, and we understand how very soon it tends to be always lost or lost to deforestation.

Consistently we're encompassed by incredible cures that go unnoticed. For instance, when we begin focusing, we can discover many distinctive "weeds"— in fields, along roadways and railroad tracks, or even in our terraces—that are fit for performing ponders for our health.

For the main occupants of this landmass, the Native Americans, nature was their drug store. They were good friends with many healing plants, grasses, and herbs. Native Americans additionally perceived the healing forces inside their bodies and treated them with extraordinary regard. They felt that the ability to heal was a blessing endowed to them by the Creator and accepted that human force and quality originated from Mother Earth and every single living thing.

Doubtlessly those progresses in clinical science have tremendously affected our lives. Individuals are living longer, healthier lives than at any time in recent memory. In any case, a portion of the advantages of current prescriptions might be balanced by their expenses. Present-day drugs are costly, in dollars, however, potentially regarding our drawn-out health. That is because, as compelling as medications can be most work by driving the body to react in specific manners, as opposed to by calling upon the body's own regular healing forces. Utilizing medications can place the body in an aloof, subordinate, and at last, weakened state.

Consider what happens when you have a disease. The advanced methodology is to take an anti-infection, which slaughters the microorganisms that are making you wiped out. In the short run, this is a reasonable arrangement, yet the body is presented to billions of microscopic organisms consistently. In the long haul, it's a losing fight. Anti-infection agents, albeit essential for battling a few diseases, are just brief protection. They don't enable the body to reinforce their own protections and oppose future diseases.

Native healers adopted an altogether extraordinary strategy. The best cures, in their view, were those that enabled the body to deal with itself, as opposed to just offering transitory help. They likewise profoundly had faith in an otherworldly segment to healing—that petition, representation, and an assortment of healing functions reinforced the body just as the brain and feelings, making recuperation a lot simpler.
Today, an expanding number of standard specialists are supporting this psyche body association. It's taken several years. However, the astuteness and experience of Native Americans are presently on the front line of current clinical consideration. Undoubtedly, the ongoing flood in "alternative" healing strategies and the utilization of petition to heal harkens back to Native American strategies: herbs and other supposed "regular" cures, representation, reflection, and the sky is the limit from there.

Numerous individuals are amazed to figure out how refined Native Americans truly were. Frequently, history presents these wise, natural individuals in a constrained light. Although the facts demonstrate that Native Americans were talented trackers, device creators, and warriors, their blessings were more wide-running than that. Up to this point, little has been said of their noteworthy gifts as healers.
Among the early settlers, Native Americans were notable for apparently inexplicable healing accomplishments. Yet, archaeologists recorded not many of these accounts, most likely

in light of racial bias and the conviction that Native Americans were "savages."

Accounts of Native American clinical ability kept on coursing by listening in on others' conversations and were recorded in frontier journals and diaries. Today, we're ready to peruse direct records from the most punctual pioneers about what the Native Americans had the option to accomplish.

In 1650, the Dutch pilgrim Adrian Van Donck composed of the high respect early pioneers had for Native American healers: "The Indians realize how to fix hazardous and risky injuries and bruises by roots, leaves, and other easily overlooked details."

Afterward, in 1714, John Lawson wrote in his History of North Carolina: "Among all the disclosures of America by the French and Spaniards, I wonder why none of them was as kind to the world as to have kept a list of the ailments they found the natives ready to fix."

Indeed, even doctors of the time were intrigued. During a gathering of the Philadelphia Medical Society in the winter of 1798, Dr. Benjamin S. Barton, a University of Pennsylvania botanist and clinical educator stated: "These individuals, albeit down and out of the lights of science, have found the properties of the absolute most endless prescriptions with which we are familiar today."

As far as it matters for them, the Native Americans were extremely mindful of the significance of their clinical blessings. Life around then was tough and troublesome, and they perceived that their endurance relied upon information on the regular world. "The Indians," composed the French voyager Jean-Bernard Boss in 1762, "esteem their therapeutic herbs more than all the gold of Mexico or Peru."

These soonest occupants of the North American landmass were a long way relatively revolutionary in their utilization of therapeutic plants, yet besides, in the manner in which they lived. When the washing was viewed as a hazardous practice, for instance, the Native Americans would dive into freezing water in the coldest climate to purge their bodies. They were solid and fit and their physical continuance astonished the Europeans. As per one early record, "These individuals are a strong and lively sort, of a hopeful disposition, honorable composition and unacquainted with a considerable number of the sicknesses that beset the Europeans."

The primary concern? Early Native Americans were living confirmation that their lifestyle was health-giving, to a great extent, because of the intensity of the health insider facts you'll discover in this book. In these pages, you'll find how the Native Americans utilized herbs to heal wounds and treat diseases, and as regular tonics to keep up their essentialness and quality. You'll additionally figure out how they consolidated otherworldliness with herbal sound medication by utilizing thoughtful methods, ceremonies, move, and music to accomplish great health.
Albeit a genuinely complete manual for Native American healing, this book speaks to just a small amount of the tremendous number of healing strategies and substances the Native Americans utilized each day. There were around 500 clans in North America before the appearance of the European pilgrims, and each had its services, practices, and convictions. Frequently, clans shared their insight into healing herbs or strategies with one another. The cures you'll discover here were among the most across the board. They are additionally the cures that are the least demanding to adjust for our utilization today, just as those cutting edge sciences have seen as the best.

The otherworldly segment of Native American healing has made reading their strategies hard for researchers now and again—hard to quantify and hard to comprehend completely. In the Native American view, health was something other than a physical state; it likewise relied upon an individual's internal agreement with the forces of nature. Native Americans accepted that neglecting to show sufficient regard for Mother Earth and the effects that made her could negatively affect physical health. In his book American Indian Medicine, student of history Virgil J. Vogel noticed that this way to deal with health "generally works in a domain of reality unfamiliar toward the Western brain."

Maybe it's less outside than it used to be. An ever-increasing number of individuals today have started to comprehend and acknowledge purported "alternative" frameworks of healing, and science is supporting them up. Consider dream treatment. Generally utilized among Native Americans to ease shrouded passionate strife, it's fundamentally the same as strategies used by current analysts. The cadenced serenades and melodic ceremonies of Native Americans share a lot of practice speaking with sleep-inducing systems utilized today. Also, the perspiration lodges used by these native individuals were the precursors of the steam rooms, saunas, and whirlpool showers in the present health clubs and clinical offices.

Native Americans are maybe most famous for their comprehension of the healing forces of plants, another region where they were a long way relatively revolutionary. Therapeutic herbs are presently a billion-dollar business. A considerable number of Americans use herbs, and an expanding number of doctors are suggesting them for their patients. Researchers have found in labs what Native Americans realized a considerable amount of years prior—that inside the universe of plants are an excellent regular drug store. A large number of the medications we use today contain ingredients almost indistinguishable from those found in nature.

A significant number of our remedies are necessarily manufactured adaptations of herbal concentrates that Native Americans utilized with extraordinary achievement. Anti-inflammatory medicine, for instance, which keeps on astounding specialists with its adequacy and flexibility, is artificially like pain murdering mixes found in the bark of the willow tree. Medications used to treat conditions, for example, diabetes and coronary illness likewise have their causes in Native American herbal mastery. As indicated by Virgil J. Vogel, "Even in similarly ongoing occasions, Indian disclosures have helped open new outskirts in the clinical history."

How to Utilize this Book

Here's the way to utilize this book most viably to bring these disclosures into your own life. To start with, look under individual instructions, "The Native American Pharmacy" to discover depictions of everyday Native American uses for a wide assortment of herbs and healing practices. These are accommodated their verifiable enthusiasm, alongside any current logical discoveries that, by and large, help their adequacy. At that point, in "Making It Work for You," you'll find how to apply Native American healing information to your health concerns today. Common diseases are recorded one after another in order, and a significant number of these customary cures have been adjusted for use at home to ease side effects or to speed healing. None of these cures ought to supplant expeditious and proper treatment by a doctor or other health care supplier, so check with your primary care physician first.

The tale of Native American healing is something beyond intriguing. It offers a framework for healing that is as helpful and down to earth for some health issues today as it was previously. There's significantly more medication in nature than the more significant part of us understand. From the antibacterial activity of the mint in your nursery to the muscle-mitigating unwinding of back rub to the pressure easing properties of brilliant dawn— the ability to control physical and enthusiastic health is, especially in your grasp. Here may you locate a start.

CHAPTER 1 - Getting Started

A most troublesome aspect concerning figuring out how to utilize herbs, regardless of whether for cooking, medication, or a mix, is the sheer number of them. You choose to begin finding out about herbs and are confronted with many new plants, some with peculiar names that you've never heard. By what means will you ever get familiar with those plants without befuddling a harmful carbon copy? In what capacity will you realize those new terms and blends? Where does one by any chance start?

The most significant thing to recall is that most botanists utilize ten or fewer herbs 90 percent of the time. Becoming more acquainted with each or two truly well, in turn, can have a considerable effect. It's the equivalent with wild nourishment scavenging. Think about all the vegetables accessible to us. What number of do you genuinely eat, however? For a great many people, that is near ten. Including three or four wild vegetables extends the sense of taste hugely.
Start by perusing a couple of field guides; winter is a fantastic time to survey them. I expect by spring you'll have a couple of herbs that you'll be on edge to discover and utilize. You'll realize what sort of landscape it tends to be found in, what it would resemble from separation and very close, and what types of plants may be discovered close by.

One of the simple initial ones I explored was clashing. I needed to utilize the natural vines and lively red and orange berries to make a wreath. I was sure that it would be in our woods someplace, so off I went, into the cold late-fall air to look. It only must be in there. After about 60 minutes, the time had come to surrender and reconsider the arrangement. Heading home, my foot slipped on the lofty, wet bank of the spring, and I slid down into the shallow water. Taking hold of presented tree roots to move out, I looked down at the earth close to my hands and roared with laughter, seeing clashing berries spread surrounding me. Reclining to look into, I noticed that the vines were high up in the trees, a lot further up than I'd looked previously. The examination had not allowed me to down.

The next year, chamomile got my attention. The year after that, it was elderberry. Thus it went. Springtime will discover a genuine threat on the roadways; I've been known to terrify friends with shouts of acknowledgment and jump from a not so much halted vehicle at seeing a field of trillium.

I suggest discovering a couple of new plants every year. Discover them, sit with them, and watch them all through the developing season. Use them. Cause them into each sort of readiness you to can think about that bodes well. Cook with them; make them into a balm, a tincture, a tea, a shower mix, or syrup. Have a go at utilizing the several valuable pieces of the plant and looking at the characteristics you find. As it were, become more acquainted with them all together so you could discover them out of the loop by their fragrance, developing propensity, and neighbours. When you know them, they will be a piece of your herbal collection until the end of time.

Responsible Wild Crafting

There are a couple of things to consider when social affair plants from nature.
Be sure beyond a shadow of a doubt in your plant identification. Take close to you need, and never gather if there isn't a plentiful stockpile of the plant. Indeed, even in bounty, take close to one-fourth of the stand, cutting so that the plant will re-become if conceivable. Roots ought to be made with the most utmost

consideration, and if there are seeds that are not your goal, return them to the ground. In my yard, dandelion, violets, and chickweed, when reaped, are pervasive to such an extent this isn't vital, however until you comprehend what needs preservation, practice limitation.

To find out about the endangered plants rundown and disregard the battling ones. You can discover this data at United Plant Savers, www.unitedplantsavers.org.
Stay at least 100 feet (30 m) over from streets and railroad tracks. On the off chance that you've at any point viewed a snowplow toss day off, realize it indeed ventures. There are likewise issues of fumes, overflow, and concoction splashing to decrease weeds by nearby wards: the more distant away, the better.

Getting authorization from the landowner is the best activity. Taking into account that what you need will, as a rule, be a weed, it is uncommon to be turned down. Indeed, even on account of old natural product trees or restorative trees, most landowners will be liberal. It additionally allows you to see if they have been treated with any synthetic substances that you don't need.
Let another person do the driving so you can concentrate on distinguishing plants you pass. Appreciate viewing the verdant arousing outside the window, and plot your next wildcrafting experience.

The Native American Herbal Medicines

It is 1536. Three ships under the order of French traveller Jacques Cartier sit unmoving in the solidified waters of the St. Lawrence River, close to the present-day city of Montreal. About a fourth of the 110-man group has as of now passed on from scurvy, an infection later demonstrated to be brought about by a lack of vitamin C. Also, more keep on capitulating. Regardless of the cataclysm, Cartier had a fortunate turn of events. Seeing the pulverization, a Native American boss named Domagaia requested his allies to start assembling and baking the appendages of a close-by tidy tree. Taken care of a dying man, the sharp tea breathed life into them back.

It was an additional 200 years before a British maritime specialist found that the solution for scurvy was vitamin C, a supplement found in numerous organic products, vegetables, and native plants, including tidy. Vitamin C is additionally rich in the adrenal organs of moose and deer—Native American delights. Native Americans didn't think about vitamin C or the logical reasons for the ailment; however, their insight into common fixes appeared to be mysterious to white pilgrims— and in light of current circumstances. Researchers have discovered that in excess of 200 plants generally utilized by Native Americans contain therapeutic mixes. Truth be told, a portion of our most usually utilized medications contain dynamic ingredients found in plants that Native Americans knew and utilized—the headache medicine like mixes in willow is an ideal model.

What was the mystery of these individuals who, with no clinical preparation in the advanced sense, knew precisely which plants to use for healing?

Native Americans relied upon nature for their endurance, says history specialist Virgil J. Vogel. The highly esteemed being cautious onlookers. They concentrated on how plants developed, where they flourished, and how they influenced creatures that ate them. More than a large number of years, and through much experimentation, they amassed colossal stores of information.

It wasn't just their forces of perception that made Native Americans such equipped healers. They were helped, they accepted, by a capacity to speak with plants about their healing forces. This may sound implausible today; however, it goes to the core of Native American healing way of thinking. They accepted that plants heal by empowering individuals to get one with Mother Nature. The life-power that travels through the foundations of dandelion was believed to be a similar life-power that travels through us. Furthermore, this power could be felt and comprehended by anybody persistent and mindful enough to tune in.

"The Native American healer accumulates herbs with a veritable sentiment of trade starting with one part of creation then onto the next," clarify Gaea and Shandor Weiss in their book Native American Healing Traditions. "The healer views plants as family members, in this sense, calling them 'medication individuals' accepted to be injected with a similar vitality as all other living things known to mankind."

Absurd? Not when you consider that "our bodies are made of similar components, minerals, and living intensifies that are found in the remainder of the common world," state the Weisses. "For each need or irregularity, consequently, there are plants that can supply the missing elements."

This sort of reasoning could be hard for pioneers to acknowledge, however botanists, students of history, and pharmacologists who have considered Native American healing point to clear proof that the early Native Americans knew precisely what they were doing. Regardless of whether plants heal for "profound" reasons is nearly irrelevant. It doesn't change the way that these plants do heal, and for reasons that are additionally totally sound and can be demonstrated in the research facility.

Researcher's gauge that in excess of 25 percent of the medications being used today contain dynamic ingredients either gotten from or synthetically like those found in plants. Cancer medications, for example, tamoxifen, and the heart tranquilize digitalis, and pain executioners, for example, morphine and ibuprofen are only a couple of instances of present-day prescriptions that have their underlying foundations in nature.

In this manner, there's nothing otherworldly about the herbal fixes utilized by Native Americans. Their sharp powers of perception and their responsibility to giving this information to people in the future made the disclosure of several intense cures sane, yet practically inescapable. Today, a great deal of current science backs many "regular" cures, the aftereffect of extraordinary examination by at first doubtful specialists who got persuaded by the mind-boggling proof they found.
Native Americans are accepted to have utilized in excess of 500 healing herbs. In the accompanying pages, we'll take a gander at those demonstrated to be safe, powerful, and promptly accessible today. You'll figure out how to prepare and use them and for which conditions. Although the cures here represent just a small amount of the Native Americans' vast knowledge, one or maybe a few of them might be only the healing insider facts you've been searching for.

CHAPTER 2 - Native American Herbs

Aloe
Aloe vera

Some of the time called an "emergency treatment pack with roots," it's among the most well-known herbs in America today. Aloe was first utilized by Native Americans in Florida and the south-western United States. It before long got known as a skin cure without equivalent, and its notoriety spread rapidly.

Native Americans utilized aloes to speed the healing of consumes and wounds, and furthermore as a treatment for creepy crawly chomps, parasitic diseases, frostbites, dermatitis, dry skin, and toxic substance ivy. Today, many skin items contain separate from this astonishing herb, and all things considered. Research has indicated that aloe encourages skin cells to recover, making it perfect for treating skin issues of assorted types. It likewise might be compelling for treating gum ailment, skin inflammation, colitis (irritation of the internal organ), and ulcers. As a liniment, it can help treat the aggravation of joint pain. Taken inside, it's additionally been utilized for facilitating obstruction. Since the unadulterated sap of the aloe plant makes a cooling, healing treatment for minor cuts, scratches, and consumes, numerous individuals, keep an aloe plant developing on their kitchen window ledges for snappy alleviation.

Physical Characteristics

Aloe is a desert flora like the plant that stands one to two feet high. It has thick, glossy, light green leaves, which are, to some degree, thorny along the edges.

Where Found

Aloe favors warm, semi-tropical conditions, yet it's a versatile plant. Presently found in many pieces of the nation, it is regularly developed inside. It ought to be watered sparingly and not given a lot of suns.

Strategies For Use

The least difficult and best approach to utilize aloe is to remove an area of one leaf and press it to discharge the thick, gel-like sap. Apply the gel to influenced regions of the skin. You can purchase aloe separates, which are planned for inside use, in health nourishment stores or herb shops. In any case, don't take aloe inside without checking with a specialist. Inside use ought to likewise be abstained from during pregnancy and bosom taking care of.

Bearberry
Arctostaphylos

Have you at any point thought about what Native Americans really put in their peace pipes? Primarily tobacco, obviously, yet in addition a touch of bearberry. This herb has gentle narcotic impacts, and it was regularly smoked during inborn committees, perhaps as a method for cultivating companionship and accord among innate pioneers. Bearberry (named for the energy bears appeared for the natural product) is in excess of a mellow sedative. It's additionally a strong diuretic and germicide. Native Americans utilized it to treat kidney stones and urinary tract diseases.

Throughout the years, cultivators have found numerous different uses for bearberry. As per The Complete Medicinal Herbal by Penelope Ody, teas produced using bearberry can help treat a condition called prostatic hypertrophy, or augmentation of the prostate organ. Ladies, in some cases, use bearberry during overwhelming menstrual periods or for uterine or vaginal contaminations. The herb seems to expand the body's yield of insulin, and it might be useful in treating a few types of diabetes.

Bearberry has numerous different uses too. Taken in little portions, it might be useful for treating looseness of the bowels; in bigger sums, it might help mitigate clogging. Weakened, it tends to be utilized as a mouthwash for treating mouth ulcers and gum aggravation. Applied as a cream, it can assist ease with burning from the sun and skin contaminations. Bearberry is an astringent, which implies it makes the skin fix. As per botanist David Hoffmann, this mellow urinary tract disinfectant is helpful for treating a few instances of bed-wetting in youngsters.

Physical Characteristics

Bearberry is a bush-like evergreen that develops low to the ground in a thick, tangled mass. It has urn-molded flowers, typically white, however here and there red-tinged, which sprout from June through September. The plant creates berries throughout the winter; however the leaves hold therapeutic properties. These ought to be reaped in the fall for the greatest quality.

Where Found

Bearberry is generally agreeable in dry sandy soil. It has an enormous range and is found from Canada to New Jersey and west right to northern California.

Strategies For USE

Bearberry can be taken inside as a tea, made by soaking one to two teaspoons of dried leaves for 10 to 15 minutes in some high temp water. You can likewise utilize bearberry as a douche, mouthwash, or germ-free by following a similar formula and permitting the fluid to cool to internal heat level.

Dark Cohosh
Cimicifuga racemose

Ladies, observe: If herbs could be blamed for sexual predisposition, dark cohosh would be blameworthy as charged. Named the "female fortifier," dark cohosh has been appeared to diminish hot flashes, sweating, headache, vertigo, heart palpitations, and tinnitus, or ringing in the ears—every single normal side effect of menopause. The herb has been so compelling in calming menopausal issues, truth be told, that a few specialists trust it might be a worthy alternative to traditional hormone substitution treatment.

Dark cohosh might be compelling for regarding other female issues also. Native Americans utilized it to assuage excruciating or postponed feminine cycle and troublesome labor—the last because of the herb's capacity to loosen up the muscles of the uterine dividers.

Dark cohosh wasn't utilized distinctly by ladies, be that as it may. Native Americans trusted it could likewise help assuage joint pain pain and the inconvenience of sicknesses, for example, red fever and smallpox, just as an assortment of respiratory issues, including challenging hack.

Physical Characteristics

Dark cohosh, which is otherwise called "bugbane" since it repulses creepy crawlies, is a tall, effortless plant with slender, blue-green leaves and long, white flowers that sprout from July through August. The greater part of the therapeutic properties lives in the roots, which are best reaped in the fall.

Where Found

The herb develops all through the eastern United States and Canada, normally on slopes and in woods that give halfway shade.

Strategies For USE

Botanists frequently use liquor to remove the healing mixes from dark cohosh, yet it additionally performs well as a tea when saturated with boiling water. Include one teaspoonful of dried root to some water, heat to the point of boiling, and let stew for 15 minutes. Drink as frequently as three times each day.

Black Haw
Viburnum prunifolium

Here's another herb for a lady's prosperity. Even though Dr. John Brickell, an eighteenth-century clinical power, applauded black haw for its capacity to heal wounds, the herb could alleviate menstrual issues that established the best connection with Native Americans. "Black haw contains various synthetic concoctions that have been demonstrated to fill in as uterine antispasmodics or relaxants," reports botanist Douglas Shar in Backyard Medicine Chest. "The plant's capacity to calm spasms has been settled."

Herbal position James A. Duke, Ph.D., creator of The Green Pharmacy, concurs. "The bark contains at any rate four substances that help loosen up the uterus," he composes. "Black haw would be one of the primary cures I'd recommend to my girl on the off chance that she came to me griping of menstrual spasms."

This plant, additionally called "crampbark," was utilized by numerous clans to treat the distresses of pregnancy—a utilization broadly prescribed by botanists today.
Native Americans utilized Black haw for some different conditions also. It was taken as a tea to soothe heart issues, stomach agony, and the runs. The leaves of the plant were bitten and applied as glue to the skin to decrease growing brought about by contaminations and injuries.
Black haw isn't without symptoms, however. Sometimes it might bother tinnitus, or ringing of the ears, in individuals previously experiencing this condition, says Dr. Duke.

Physical Characteristics
A plant relative of the honeysuckle plant, Black haw develops as an erect, hairy bush 10 to 25 feet tall. It has dull green leaves and groups of little white flowers that sprout in the late-spring. The plant likewise bears little dark or dull blueberries. The berries are consumable, yet numerous individuals think of them as unendurably sweet.

Where Found
Black haw is found all through the majority of the United States, yet for the most part in the East from Maine to Florida. It very well may be developed from seed or from existing plants, which are usually accessible at garden focuses and from mail-request houses. You can purchase dried Black haw root bark, and all things considered health nourishment stores and herb shops.

Strategies For USE
The least demanding, best approach to utilize Black haw is as a tea. When utilizing the root, put an ounce in 16 ounces of cool water in a pot, heat to the point of boiling, and stew for 20 to 30

minutes. Strain the fluid, cool, and drink varying. Since Black haw is tedious to plan, numerous individuals pick accommodation and rather make a tea utilizing a tincture, accessible in health nourishment stores.

Corn
Zea mays

Native Americans acquainted corn with the advanced world, and it's maybe their most noteworthy commitment to our day by day slims down. In any case, corn is substantially more than a flexible and nutritious grain. It's additionally been broadly utilized for its healing forces.

Spanish voyagers in the sixteenth century revealed that Native Americans drank a drink produced using corn to treat issues with the kidneys and bladder. Antiquarians have found that a corn-based drink was utilized to treat diarrhea and acid reflux and to expand milk creation in nursing moms. Corn likewise was generally utilized by Native Americans to make poultices for skin ulcers, consumes, and growing, and corn oil was applied to ease dermatitis and dry skin. Indeed, even the cobs were utilized therapeutically. Native Americans would consume the cobs, accepting that the smoke would help ease tingling brought about by creepy crawly nibbles and toxic substance ivy.

A significant number of the customary uses for corn has been approved by present-day inquire about. Corn, particularly the "silk," has been demonstrated to have diuretic properties known to be useful in treating hypertension and contaminations of the kidneys, bladder, and urinary tract.

Just as in declaration to Native American knowledge, many skin powders today contain cornstarch since it's been appeared to help assuage skin conditions, for example, dermatitis.

Physical Characteristics

Most assortments of corn grow six to eight feet tall, contingent upon soil conditions and dampness. The plant has a thick tail, enormous splendid green leaves, and "ears" of parts secured by a multi-layered husk. Between the husk and the bits are the "silk"— fine strands of defensive material that numerous cultivators accept is the plant's most therapeutic part.

Where Found

Corn can be developed almost anyplace in North America, a more or less long plenitude of dampness and daylight. It flourishes all around treated the soil and typically expects 70 to 80 days to develop.

Strategies For Use

Corn is multi-gifted, restoratively. For interior conditions, its silk can be utilized new or dried to make a tea. Steep two teaspoons, cleaved, in boiling water. Remotely, a corn poultice can relieve minor consumes and other skin aggravations. To set up the poultice, blend dried cornmeal in with drain and apply the glue to the influenced territories.

Dandelion
Taraxacum officinale

It's as of late that dandelion has been diminished to the status of the rural nuisance. For quite a long time, dandelion positioned among the strongest natural cures. Native Americans and Europeans the same saw the dandelion as very nearly a panacea—an intense medication yet, also an exceptionally nutritious green vegetable.

Native Americans cut dandelion roots to make a topical sterile for wounds, injuries, and irritation in the mouth. They likewise prepared a tea, produced using the leaves, as a mellow purgative and stomach related guide. The tea was accepted to have diuretic properties and was utilized to "purge" the kidneys, bladder, liver, and spleen.

As nourishment, dandelion is difficult to beat. The leaves and roots were eaten crude or bubbled. Exceptionally nutritious, dandelion provided Native Americans with goodly measures of iron, potassium, phosphorus, and vitamins A, B, C, and D. They even ate the dandelion flowers, which are wealthy in lecithin. This significant supplement has been appeared to help treat an assortment of liver issues.

Researchers have since found that dandelion is extremely plentiful in calcium, containing 200 milligrams of this mineral in 10 grams (around 33% of an ounce) of dried leaves. This recommends dandelion might be extremely useful in forestalling osteoporosis, a genuine bone-debilitating condition that influences ladies after menopause. What's more, calcium isn't the main explanation dandelion is useful for the bones. It likewise contains boron and silicon; significant follow minerals that assume significant jobs in the bone-saving procedure.

The examination is the starter, yet a few investigations propose that dandelion may even be useful in forestalling Alzheimer's disease, because of its adequate measures of lecithin and choline. In research center investigations, these substances have been appeared to help improve memory.

Cultivators today keep on suggesting dandelion as a diuretic. Since it frees the assortment of overabundance water, it can "flush" the kidneys and bladder, which may help keep these organs liberated from the disease.

Dandelion has such a significant number of restorative uses that it's practically difficult to show them all. Studies have indicated that dandelion tea can help alleviate pneumonia, bronchitis, and other upper respiratory issues. Since it goes about as a diuretic, it might be useful in diminishing growing brought about by hyper-extends or limited contaminations. A few botanists prescribe everyday utilization of dandelion "milk," the smooth sap from leaves and stems, as a sheltered and compelling method for expelling corns and moles, says Dr. Duke.

Physical Characteristics

Dandelion's particular appearance makes it difficult to miss. Its leaves are spiked or tooth-molded, which clarifies its name—the word originates from the French imprint de lion, signifying "tooth of the lion." It flowers into a solitary, splendid yellow bloom, which later transforms into a round puff of cushy headed seeds that go airborne, as modest parachutes, with the scarcest breeze.

Where Found

Dandelion is perhaps the hardiest plant on earth, as cultivators and yard buffs from northern Canada right toward the southern tip of Mexico can verify. The plant can put down roots even in the harshest atmospheres and rockiest soils. Late-winter and pre-winter are the best occasions to gather the leaves and roots, which become excessively severe during the warmth of summer—however, summer is the best time for reaping the flowers. It's ideal for getting them at their fullest bloom, just before they go to seed.

Strategies For USE

Since dandelion leaves are delicate and carefully unpleasant, they're prized as a serving of mixed greens green. (As a little something extra, the leaves are unfathomably plentiful in vitamin A, containing considerably a greater amount of this supplement than carrots do.) Dandelion can be eaten crude or arranged by boiling or sautéing. Since the leaves do have an unpleasant note, numerous individuals include a touch of improvement. Among the Pennsylvania Dutch, for instance, dandelions are regularly presented with a dressing produced using juice vinegar and sugar, and maybe a little bacon. The roots are best when bubbled or heated, and the flowers can be changed into a delicate delicacy, tasting something like mushrooms, when seared in spread or oil. All pieces of the plant can be evaporated and put away for a year without losing their therapeutic properties.

Echinacea
Echinacea angustifolia

Echinacea has gotten amazingly famous as of late for assisting with subduing colds and other upper respiratory diseases. By and by, Native American healers were in front of all of us. As indicated by botanist Melvin Gilmore, echinacea was utilized "as a solution for additional afflictions than some other plant."

Paul Lee, an originator of the Platonic Academy of Herbal Studies, calls echinacea "our driving herb on the rundown of immuno-energizers." What this implies is that echinacea can fortify the safe framework, improving the body ready to oppose contamination causing microscopic organisms and infections. Botanist David Hoffmann says echinacea "is powerful against both bacterial and viral assaults, less by executing these life forms, however by supporting the body's own regular safeguards against them."

Hoffmann and different cultivators suggest echinacea for upper respiratory contaminations, including laryngitis and tonsillitis. It might likewise assuage aggravation in the mucous films of the nose and sinuses. At the point when utilized in a mouthwash, echinacea might be useful in treating ailments of the gums.

The healing mixes in echinacea are found in the roots. Research has indicated that they contain caffeine corrosive glycoside, a substance that responds with different synthetic concoctions in the body to encourage wound healing. The roots likewise contain a substance that battles microorganisms and another that battles infections by hindering a catalyst they use to separate cell dividers. Utilized in moisturizer structure, echinacea seems to speed the healing of cuts and injuries.

Physical Characteristics
Echinacea is perpetual that looks, especially like dark, peered toward Susan. It has a bristly stem and huge, bushy leaves that decrease to a point toward the end. It develops to a stature of around three feet and has an enormous, pinkish, daisy-like flower at the top.

Where Found
Echinacea generally develops in open fields and alongside the road in the focal fields states west of Ohio. It's an astoundingly strong plant that can be developed from seed in about any prolific, very much depleted soil. Concentrates of the herb are generally accessible at drug stores, herb shops, and health nourishment stores.

Strategies For Use
The core of echinacea's therapeutic forces is the root. The roots ought to be gathered late in the fall after a few hard pieces of ice. They ought to be cleaned, dried for half a month, at that point

ground into a coarse powder for making teas. To make a tea, include a couple of teaspoons of powdered herb to some boiling water. Let stew for 15 minutes, cool, and drink varying, up to three times each day. The tea can likewise be utilized remotely for treating cuts, consumes, and skin inflammation—or as a mouthwash to treat gum issues. A few cultivators prescribe swishing with the tea to mitigate sore throats.

Fennel
Foeniculum vulgare

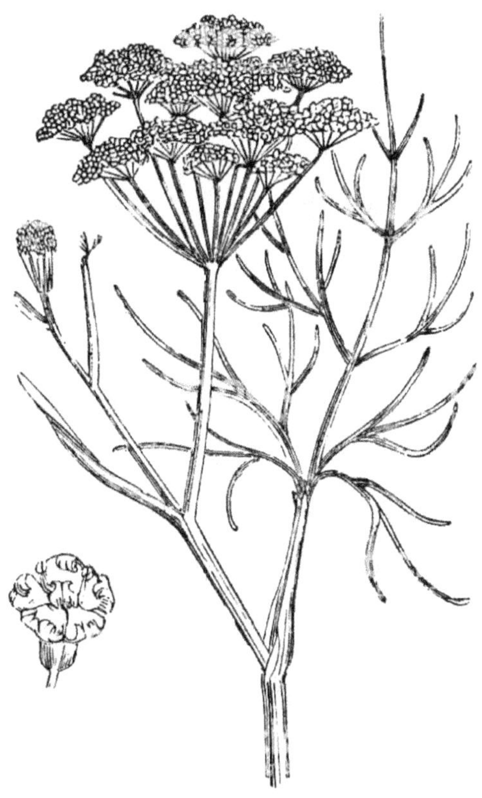

Since fennel is prestigious for improving awful breath and diminishing intestinal gas, it was famous among Native Americans for reasons that probably been social just as therapeutic. It has additionally relieved hacks and quieted heartburn. Fennel can be utilized as a pack to diminish conjunctivitis, an irritation of the eyelid, or applied as a poultice to treat muscle and joint agony. Nursing moms drank fennel tea to expand their creation of bosom milk.

Fennel's therapeutic notoriety has just become throughout the years, and cultivators suggest it for an assortment of conditions. As per botanist David Hoffmann, "Fennel is a decent stomach and intestinal cure which diminishes fart and colic while likewise animating assimilation and craving." According to natural power David B. Mowrey, Ph.D., "Fennel is particularly compelling against tooting in grown-ups," in this manner demonstrating by and by those Native American healers knew what they were doing.

Physical Characteristics

Fennel is a solid enduring that develops to around five feet. It has a splendid green, sparkly stem, and padded plantlike leaves. It produces little; splendid yellow flowers in bunches taking after upside-down umbrellas. The flowers offer an approach to seeds, which hold the vast majority of the herb's restorative forces.

Where Found

Fennel is native to the Mediterranean district, yet spread rapidly through North America, starting in California and bit by bit moving east. It loves full sun and all around depleted soil, and does well in many nurseries.

Strategies For USE

Botanists generally prescribe utilizing fennel seeds to make a tea. Include two teaspoons of marginally squashed seeds to some boiling water, let represent 10 minutes, strain, and drink as regularly as three times each day.

To forestall tooting, drink some fennel tea thirty minutes before eating. For outer use, set up the tea, let cool, at that point apply where required.

Fennel seeds are mainstream as breath mints, which is the reason a few eateries keep a bowlful close to the registration register. Furthermore, oil got from fennel, accessible in health nourishment stores, can be utilized to make an alleviating rub for muscle and joint pain.

Aside from its therapeutic uses, fennel is prized in the kitchen. The seeds have a rich, sweet flavor and are normally used to season fish, soups, stews, plates of mixed greens, and bread. You can likewise eat the fennel bulb as a vegetable, preparing or boiling it until delicate.

Even though fennel is commonly sheltered, it is known to be a uterine energizer and ought to be maintained a strategic distance from high dosages during pregnancy.

Garlic
Allium

On the off chance that you think garlic is well known as a healing herb today, it was much more sizzling previously. It has been utilized by societies worldwide for a great many years, and Native Americans were no exemption. They utilized garlic to treat snakebites and wounds. They arranged it as a syrup for respiratory diseases, blockage, and colds—and, in what must be portrayed as a significant clinical achievement, they found that garlic could fix scurvy. Scurvy is a genuine, possibly deadly sickness brought about by a lack of vitamin C—and garlic, it turns out, is a rich wellspring of this significant supplement.

As of late, garlic has been the focal point of several logical examinations. Specialists have found, for instance, that when garlic is squashed, it discharges a substance called allicin, which has antiviral and antibacterial properties. It has additionally been appeared to help battle diseases brought about by parasites and yeast. It's even dynamic against influenza infections.

Among its many healing mixes, garlic contains unpredictable oils that a few analysts accept can help away from lungs and bronchial containers of clog. Garlic likewise contains sulfur mixes, which, alongside giving garlic its particular smell, might be lethal to intestinal parasites. Sometime before specialists recognized these mixes, Native Americans were utilizing garlic to free individuals of worms and different parasites.

In probably the most energizing examination as of late, researchers have discovered that garlic seems to help diminish the danger of cardiovascular failures. It does this in three different ways: by bringing down circulatory strain, decreasing degrees of destructive LDL cholesterol in the blood, and lessening the propensity of blood to shape perilous, conceivably heart-blocking clusters. Studies propose that as meager as one clove of new garlic daily might be sufficient to deliver these defensive impacts.

New research recommends garlic's advantages go significantly further. It seems, by all accounts, to be useful for individuals with diabetes, cerebral headache pains, cardiovascular arrhythmia (unpredictable pulses), and discontinuous claudication (poor course brought about by a narrowing of corridors in the legs). A few specialists hypothesize that garlic may secure against specific types of disease also.

Physical Characteristics
Garlic plants have long, limited, green leaves that develop to around two feet in stature. Generally natural is the garlic bulb, which comprises of 4 to 15 firmly stuffed cloves.

Where Found

Garlic is thought to have started in southern Siberia however is currently found in many pieces of the world. Garlic does best in rich, profound, and wet (however all around depleted) soil that gets a lot of suns.

Strategies For USE
The most straightforward approach to appreciate the plentiful health advantages of garlic is to eat it, ideally crude. Crude garlic is a procured taste, obviously, and a few people discover it excessively overpowering. Luckily, garlic holds its therapeutic properties when utilized in different structures. For instance:

Garlic tea: Slash or squash a few cloves of garlic and let steep in some water for six to eight hours. You can drink the tea for mitigating cold or influenza side effects, or you can utilize it as a wash for treating an irritated throat.

Garlic syrup: Add a pound of garlic to a quart of boiling water. Expel from the warmth and let represent 12 hours; at that point, add enough sugar to accomplish a syrup-like consistency. A few people include honey or vinegar overflowed with fennel or caraway seeds to improve the taste. Garlic syrup can be utilized to ease hacks. At the point when taken in modest quantities consistently, it might fortify resistance and help the heart.
Garlic oil: Cut or squash a clove of garlic include about a tablespoon of olive oil and warmth quickly. At that point, strain the oil and store in a dim, stopper container. You can utilize a few drops to facilitate an ear infection.

Ginseng
Panax quinquefolias

Ginseng has been utilized for more than 5,000 years, in America, however, around the globe. Native Americans considered ginseng sacrosanct, and warriors once in a while conveyed it like a four-leaf clover. It was as a medication; nonetheless, that ginseng made its most prominent imprint. Native Americans utilized ginseng to treat migraines, cramps, fevers, heaving, hacks, cuts, the brevity of breath, and fruitlessness in ladies. The herb was thought to increment sexual want in both genders, which may clarify why one clan considered it the "man root."

Researchers accept that ginseng's notoriety for expanding sexual ability is, to be magnanimous, fairly exaggerated. Nonetheless, numerous cultivators feel that ginseng increases imperativeness, causing individuals to feel more grounded and progressively fiery. They consider ginseng an "adaptogen," implying that it encourages the body to adjust to worries of numerous types, physical just as passionate.

Studies recommend that ginseng reduces exhaustion and improve athletic execution. It likewise might be useful for animating the safe framework, improving memory, diminishing sorrow, and, in people with diabetes, improving the capacity to endure sugars.

Physical Characteristics

Ginseng has a slim, single stem that isolates into a few side stems bearing leaves in groups of four or five each. The herb develops to somewhere in the range of one and two feet in stature and starts from a huge, meaty, white taproot, which is the place the majority of the therapeutic mixes live. More seasoned plants bear little green flowers and brilliant red berries.

Where Found

Because of its prevalence and worth, ginseng is, to some degree, uncommon today. It develops wild in obscure zones and hardwood timberlands running from eastern Canada to Maine and Minnesota, and southward into the mountain locales of the Carolinas and Georgia.

Strategies For USE

Ginseng is generally utilized as a tea, made by including a teaspoon of powdered root to some boiling water. Let represent 10 or 15 minutes, at that point, strain, and drink at the earliest opportunity. Crude ginseng isn't in every case simple to discover, yet health nourishment stores and herb shops normally convey ginseng separates.

Ginseng is an extremely supportive herb; however it's conceivable to get an overdose of something that is otherwise good. Taking an excessive amount of may cause headache, hyperactivity, anxiety, melancholy, and a sleeping disorder.

Goldenrod
Solidago

Native Americans believed goldenrod to help heal a wide assortment of issues, and all aspects of the plant were utilized. The roots were made into poultices to treat bubbles and consume, orbit to calm toothaches. The flowers were squashed to make a salve for mitigating honey bee stings and diminishing confined swellings. The tea produced using the leaves was utilized to treat conditions running from asthma and colic to headache and measles. Goldenrod was likewise utilized as a disinfectant, and smoke from the consuming herb was thought to restore individuals who had fallen oblivious.

Native Americans frequently utilized goldenrod for bladder, gallbladder, and kidney issues, and it's these applications that have best withstood the examination of present-day science. Goldenrod contains a compound called leiocarposide, a strong diuretic. German doctors frequently suggest goldenrod for forestalling and treating kidney stones and gallstones, just as yeast and urinary tract contaminations.

Physical Characteristics
There are over 130 assortments of this solid lasting. The stems ordinarily develop to three to seven feet, and most assortments have little yellow flowers that develop in elliptical bunches. Goldenrod has a charming smell and anise-like taste. A few people add goldenrod to different herbs to make them progressively agreeable.

Where Found
Goldenrod is found all through North America, as a rule in open fields and alongside the road. It prefers full sun; however, it can develop in about any very much depleted soil.

Strategies For USE
The most straightforward approach to utilize goldenrod is as a tea. Include five teaspoons of dried flowers or leaves to some boiling water. Let remain until cool, at that point serve. It's ideal for taking goldenrod between suppers, three or four times each day.
Goldenrod is sheltered, yet a few people might be adversely affected by it. Use it with caution on the off chance that you have feed fever or different hypersensitivities.

Goldenseal
Hydrastis Canadensis

Cultivator Jethro Kloss has called goldenseal "one of the most magnificent cures in the whole herbal realm." So brilliant, indeed, that the plant about got wiped out in the mid-1900s since it was collected so vigorously. In a solitary year, more than 300,000 pounds were reaped as updates on its healing forces spread from North America all through the world.

The Cherokee were the principal Native Americans to find goldenseal's therapeutic qualities, utilizing it as a germ-free to treat bolt wounds and biting on the roots to mitigate injuries in the mouth. Throughout the years, goldenseal's flexibility extended. It was taken to treat stomach related issues, for example, ulcers, colitis, clogging, and loss of hunger—utilizes that are reliable with the herb's capacity to build bile discharge from the liver, as indicated by cultivator David Hoffmann.

Goldenseal has additionally been utilized to treat ear infections, bladder diseases, colds and influenza, constant weakness, tinnitus (ringing in the ears), yeast contaminations, tonsillitis, blister, intestinal parasites, and competitor's foot.

Physical Characteristics

Goldenseal is a little, 6-to 12-inch enduring with an erect, bristly stem, maple-molded leaves, splendid red berries, and a particular light-green bloom.

Where Found

Goldenseal is essentially found in the northeastern United States. It inclines toward sodden forests, clammy valleys, and good forested countries.

Strategies For USE

Goldenseal is best taken as a tea produced using the plant's underlying foundations, which ought to be collected in the fall. Include a teaspoonful of dried, powdered root to some boiling water, permit to soak for 15 minutes, strain, and take one tablespoonful three to six times each day. The tea may likewise be utilized remotely to treat cuts, tingling, ringworm, skin inflammation, ear infections, and conjunctivitis (aggravation of the inward surface of the eyelids).

Gravel Root
Eupatorium purpureum

Try not to let the humble name fool you. Gravel root, likewise called "joe pie weed" to pay tribute to a famous Native American healer, was held in the most noteworthy respect by both Native Americans and Europeans.

The herb gets its unordinary name from one of its unique uses: Native Americans utilized gravel root to treat bladder and kidney stones. It was likewise used to calm back agony, stiffness, stomach pain, stoppage, colds, and gout. Since it was accepted to cause abundant perspiring, it was once in a while used to "break" a fever, particularly typhoid fever. The Creek clan in the Alabama locale bubbled gravel root to make steam, which was thought to mitigate joint pains in the hips.

Gravel root is broadly utilized today in homeopathy for improving liver and kidney work, facilitating the throbs, pain, and fever that go with colds and influenza, and for clearing an upper respiratory clog. It's occasionally prescribed to ease clogging and difficult monthly cycle.

Physical Characteristics

Gravel root is an enduring that normally develops from 3 to 10 feet in tallness. It has an inflexible, halfway empty stem. Its leaves, crimped on the upper side, however delicate and smooth underneath, develop from the stem in whorls of four or five, each couple of inches. Pinkish or purple flowers molded like umbrellas show up at the highest point of the plant.

Where Found

Gravel root is found all through the greater part of North America, from Canada down to Florida. It, for the most part, develops in ripe marshes, along stream banks, and in clammy, lush regions, and bogs.

Strategies For USE

Gravel root is best gathered when its flowers open in the late summer. All aspects of the plant are restoratively dynamic, and it's typically taken as a tea. Add one to two teaspoons of dried herb to some boiling water, let steep for 10 to 15 minutes, strain, and drink as frequently as each half-hour for a cold or influenza. Use gravel root with some restraint because, in enormous sums, it very well may be lethal.

Hawthorn
Crataegus monogyna

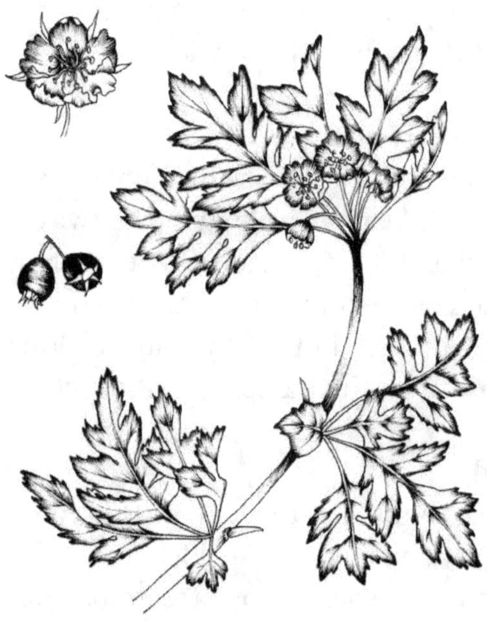

Here's a herb to hold near your heart. Albeit Native Americans utilized hawthorn to treat expanding, loose bowels, and interior dying, scientists today are progressively energized by its capacity to support cardiovascular conditions. As indicated by botanist David Hoffmann, "This herb furnishes us with outstanding amongst other tonic solutions for the entire of the heart and circulatory framework."

Specialists accept that hawthorn might be particularly helpful for treating congestive cardiovascular breakdown, a genuine, conceivably hazardous condition, says natural position James A. Duke, Ph.D. Hawthorn seems to help the heart in an assortment of ways. It can bring down cholesterol levels and help forestall the development of plaque on conduit dividers, which permits more blood and oxygen to go through the supply routes. This is basic for forestalling respiratory failures and easing angina, and the chest pains brought about by a deficiency of oxygen to the heart muscle.

Hawthorn is likewise accepted to bring down hypertension by expanding the adaptability of vein dividers. It's even been appeared to improve some heart conditions related to ailments of the liver, for example, cirrhosis and hepatitis.

Initially, just the berries of the hawthorn tree were believed to be restoratively dynamic; however later research has demonstrated that the flowers and leaves contain dynamic mixes, as well. Even though the berries are best gathered in the fall, the flowers and leaves ought to be picked in the late spring.

Physical Characteristics

Hawthorn develops as a little tree, around 25 feet high, with prickly branches and little, maple-formed leaves accompanied by little white flowers that develop in bunches. The flowers show up in spring and the brilliant red berries age in pre-fall or late-summer.

Where Found

Hawthorn is native to Europe and Asia; however it currently develops in numerous calm areas in the United States. It's generally found along with hedgerows and amid deciduous (leaf-bearing) trees.

Strategies For USE

Since hawthorn leaves, flowers, and berries are, for the most part, restoratively dynamic, you can utilize any or every one of them to make a tea. The berries are the most promptly accessible parts, in any case, so a great many people make a berry tea, utilizing either entire berries or a hawthorn extricate. To cause a berry tea, to pour some boiling water more than two teaspoons of berries. Let represent 20 minutes, at that point,

strain and serve. You can drink the tea as regularly as three times each day.
Heart conditions are constantly genuine, be that as it may, so it's basic to initially check with your primary care physician before utilizing any herbal medicines at home.

Hops
Humulus lupulus

At the point when we consider Hops, we, as a rule, invoke pictures of foamy cups of beer and high times. Among Native Americans, in any case, bounces filled increasingly calm needs. The Mohegan clan utilized bounces blooms to make a narcotic. The blooms were dried and placed in a little sack. At the point when utilized as a cushion, it was thought to calm ear infections and toothaches and to assist individuals with resting all the more sufficiently.

Different clans bit Hops roots to make a topical antiseptic for wounds. A tea produced using the plant's leaves was utilized to treat uneasiness, a sleeping disorder, apprehensive acid reflux, ulcers, and premenstrual spasms.

Present-day inquire about has done a lot to affirm the therapeutic forces of bounces, particularly its calming characteristics. As indicated by herbal master Daniel B. Mowrey, Ph.D., "a mitigating, loosening up quiet will be experienced inside twenty to thirty minutes of ingesting the herb."

Bounces show up additionally to be successful as a stomach related guide since its extraordinary harshness "animates stomach related capacity, bile emission from the liver and the assimilation of supplements," as indicated by cultivator David Winston. Different botanists suggest Hopspoultices for facilitating joint and muscle pain.

Physical Characteristics
Hops develop as vine-like wild grapes, which can reach up to 40 feet in stature. Little, yellowish-green, cone-formed flowers show up in the plant's third year of development. The flowers ought to be picked in the late-summer before completely develop and dried quickly, ideally not in the sun, to save their greatest quality.

Where Found
Hops are native to Europe yet now develop bounteously in most mild locales in the United States and Canada. Hops do best in a rich, wet soil that gets full sun.

Strategies For USE
A large portion of the therapeutic parts are in the flowers, and most botanists suggest accepting bounces as a tea. Include a teaspoonful of dried flowers to some boiling water, let represent 10 to 15 minutes, strain, and drink varying.
As a tranquilizer, it's ideal for drinking Hops tea about thirty minutes before hitting the sack—or you can have a go at placing dried flowers in a little sack and setting it underneath your head around evening time. This procedure wasn't utilized uniquely by Native Americans, by chance. President Abraham Lincoln,

upset by the Civil War, is said to have utilized a bounces cushion to enable him to rest.

The one issue with utilizing a bounces cushion is that the dried herb will stir and may keep you wakeful. Botanists suggest somewhat soaking the bounces with water, which will keep the riotous blooms somewhat calmer.

Horsetail
Equisetum

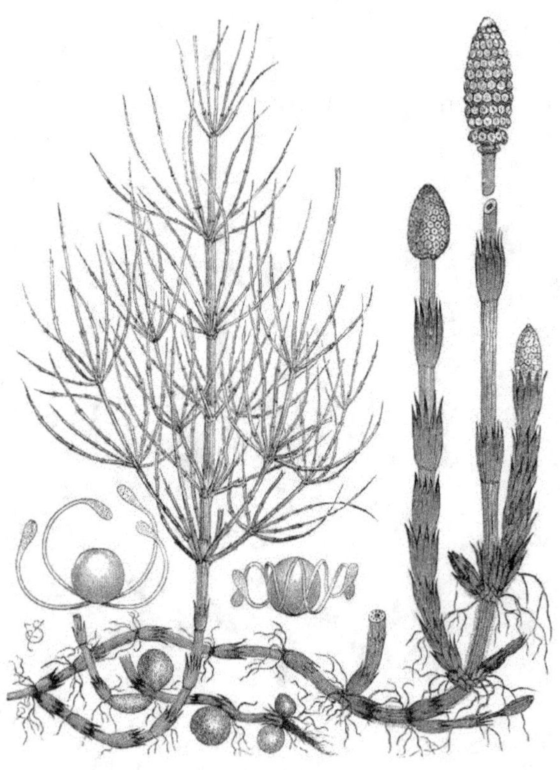

Horsetail has an astonishing history. As indicated by Gaea and Shandor Weiss, creators of Growing and Using Healing Herbs, it was one of the principle nourishment wellsprings of the plant-eating dinosaurs. It may have assumed a job in their inconceivable size. Horsetail, additionally called shave grass, is outstandingly plentiful in bone-building minerals—calcium, yet also, silicon, which adds to the development of ligament and ligaments.

The Native Americans esteemed horsetail for its bone-reinforcing and other tissue-recovering forces. It much of the time was utilized as a poultice to heal cracks and wounds, and it was taken as a tea to stop inward dying. They likewise utilized the tea to treat urinary tract contaminations, kidney issues, and ulcers.

Botanists today prescribe horsetail for fighting osteoporosis, the bone-diminishing infection that regularly happens in ladies after menopause when declining levels of estrogen lessen the body's capacity to retain calcium.

A few cultivators prescribe horsetail for treating bursitis and tendinitis. The silicon in horsetail may help reinforce ligament and fix minor harm. What's more, they keep on prescribing horsetail for urinary tract contaminations and kidney stones, just as the development of the prostate organ, incontinence in grown-ups, and bed-wetting in youngsters.

Even though it's not something you'd anticipate from a healing herb, horsetail has another reasonable use. Due to its silicon content, the herb is marginally coarse, which makes it perfect for cleaning dishes or in any event, sanding wood!

Physical Characteristics

Horsetail shows up in two phases. In the principal stage, the plant takes after a little Christmas tree. It's about a foot high and has whorls of flaky, brilliant green branches. In the subsequent stage, the branches tumble off, leaving a desolate, olive-green, bamboo-like tail around 18 inches high.

Where Found

Horsetail is found all through North America, and it's frequently very bullish about taking over other vegetation. Search for it along roadways and railroad tracks and in wet places, for example, swamps and at the edges of lakes, streams, and lakes.

Strategies For USE

Most cultivators prescribe utilizing horsetail to make a tea. Include five teaspoons of dried herb, utilizing any piece of the plant, and a teaspoonful of sugar to a quart of boiling water. (Including sugar helps discharge the silicon.) Reduce the warmth and let stew for three hours. Strain the tea, let it cool, and take a significant piece or so a few times each day.

It's ideal to reap horsetail in the fall when the silicon content is most noteworthy.

Juniper
Juniperus communis

Native Americans so broadly utilized juniper berries for healing that the tree itself got known as "the medication tree." They utilized juniper berry tea as a diuretic for individuals with bladder diseases. The tea was additionally used to diminish vexed stomachs and as an antiseptic for purging injuries. They heated the berries to deliver steam, which was thought to assuage blockage. An oil produced using the branches and berries of the juniper tree was utilized to knead sore joints and muscles. As a little something extra, the salve was a compelling, creepy crawly repellent.

Scientists have discovered that juniper berries contain an exacerbate that seems to hinder various distinctive infections, including those that cause herpes and influenza. The berries have additionally been found to battle microorganisms, and research recommends they might be useful for joint pain too.

Physical Characteristics

An individual from the pine family, the juniper is a little tree, 10 to 25 feet high. It has meagerly needled branches and little, dull purple berries that show up during the second year of development. All pieces of the tree are restorative, yet the berries a large portion of all.

Where Found

Juniper trees are found all through North America, even in the driest and least rich soils.

Strategies For USE

To make a juniper berry tea, relax two teaspoons of new berries by absorbing them water for a couple of hours. At that point, add them to 16 ounces of boiling water and let them cook for 30 minutes. Allow the tea to cool and drink varying.

Juniper berries are dangerous when taken in huge sums or utilized for broadened timeframes. They shouldn't be utilized during pregnancy, by those with kidney issues, or by any individual who is sensitive to dust.

Lady's Slipper
Cypripedium calceolus

The lady's slipper flower is so delightful; Native American ladies regularly wore it in their hair. Notwithstanding, the herb was esteemed less for its magnificence than for its therapeutic sturdiness. Native American healers utilized lady's slipper to treat excruciating period, troublesome labor, craziness, chorea (wild, uncontrollable developments), and sleep deprivation.

One student of history detailed that lady's slipper was rumored to have given serene rest to a patient so hit with sleeping disorder even opium hadn't made a difference. As indicated by cultivator David Hoffmann, "the herb might be utilized in all pressure responses, enthusiastic strain, and tension states."

Physical Characteristics
Woman's shoe, which gets its name from its shoe-formed flower, is indisputable for its excellence alone. An individual

from the orchid family, it has enormous leaves and somewhere in the range of 1 to 12 huge, multi-hued, pocket like flowers at the top. The herb's underlying foundations are the most therapeutic part and are best accumulated in pre-fall or late-summer.

Where Found

Lady's slipper is found in the eastern United States and as far south as Georgia and Louisiana. It likewise shows up in the western conditions of Oregon and Arizona.

Strategies For USE

A lady's slipper is typically utilized as a tea to calm a sleeping disorder. Include two teaspoons of dried root to some boiling water. Let steep 10 to 15 minutes, strain, and drink as frequently as important.

Licorice
Glycyrrhiza glabra

If your endurance relied upon subtle chasing, as the Native Americans frequently did, the exact opposite thing you'd need would be a wild hack. All the quality, expertise, and readiness on the planet wouldn't help if the game could hear you hacking and hacking a mile away.

Hundreds of years before hack drops showed up in perfect little boxes; Native American clans were utilizing licorice root to relieve hacks and sore throats. As indicated by Rodale's Illustrated Encyclopedia of Herbs, "although we consider

licorice basically as a sweets seasoning, its constituents currently are being appeared to have a surprising scope of pharmacological properties."
Botanists today suggest licorice pull for such different conditions as fever, menstrual spasms, disturbed entrails, and urinary entries, respiratory infirmities, ulcers, clogging, low pulse, and influenza.

Herbal authority James Duke acclaims licorice for its healing forces. He says it might be useful for joint pain, asthma, competitor's foot, blister, gum disease, acid reflux, constant weariness, Lyme sickness, psoriasis, prostate extension, Addison's ailment, dandruff, discouragement, and even hairlessness. Research center investigations suggest that the substance that makes licorice sweet, called glycyrrhizin, may someday play a role in preventing cancer.

Physical Characteristics
The licorice plant, which can grow up to seven feet tall, has short elliptical leaves, little purple flowers, and little, reddish-brown units. The plant's foundations hold a large portion of its therapeutic worth. They branch off from a principle taproot in a tangled mass that can reach out as much as four feet down.

Where Found
Licorice is native to southern Europe and western Asia, yet now develops wild in California just as in some northwestern, Midwestern, and eastern states. It very well may be developed from seed; however, it improves when begun from cuttings, ideally root cuttings. The therapeutic strength tops during the pre-winter of the plant's third or fourth year.
Strategies For USE
For inside conditions, for example, joint pain, colds, or interminable exhaustion, licorice is generally utilized as a tea.

You can likewise utilize the tea remotely to treat skin issues. Include a teaspoonful of dried, powdered licorice root, or a teaspoonful of licorice syrup (see beneath), to some boiling water. When utilizing licorice root, let represent around 10 minutes, at that point, strain and serve. With licorice syrup, you can drink the tea when it's blended and has cooled to an agreeable temperature.

For a licorice germ-free, it's ideal for making a concentrated fluid. Include a pound of new licorice root to three pints of water and bubble until the fluid is diminished by around 33%.

As opposed to utilizing new or dried root, a few herbalists prescribe making liquorice syrup, which can be put away in a shrouded compartment in the cooler. Fill a baking dish with new or dried licorice root, spread with water, and stew in the grill or on the stovetop for three to four hours. Dispose of the roots, strain the staying fluid, include two teaspoons of honey for some fluid, and store in a cleaned compartment with a tight-fitting top. The syrup can be utilized to make licorice tea or taken undiluted, each or two tea spoonfuls, in turn, to mitigate an irritated throat, hack, or upper respiratory blockage related to colds or influenza.

Since the mixes in licorice can cause water maintenance, the herb ought not to be utilized by pregnant ladies or by anybody with heart issues, kidney complexities, or hypertension. Licorice may cause symptoms, for example, torpidity, headache, or an ascent in circulatory strain.

Magnolia
Magnolia

Scarcely any trees are as wonderful or fragrant when in sprout as the magnolia. In any case, don't let its flabbergasting charm fool you—it's incredible medication. History is loaded up with reports of fruitful medicines utilizing this fragrant tree. As per a frontier student of history, a Swedish pioneer with ulcerated leg bruises immediately recouped in the wake of being treated by a Native American who blessed the injuries with a blend of magnolia cinders and pork fat. "This evaporated the injuries which before were ceaselessly open, and the legs of the elderly person stayed sound until his demise," he composed.

Different reports recount Native Americans baking the parts of the magnolia tree to make a tea, which they used to treat colds, fever, looseness of the bowels, muscle cramps, and intestinal worms. All the more as of late, herbalists have extended the employments of magnolia tea, produced using either the bark or leaves, to treat sickness, asthma, and tobacco habit. A magnolia swish is said to be compelling for facilitating toothaches, and magnolia decoctions have been utilized as disinfectants for cuts, scratches, and other skin disturbances.

Physical Characteristics

The magnolia is a little tree, 10 to 20 feet high, with smooth grayish bark, three-to four-inch leaves, and huge pink and white flowers that sprout in mid-spring.

Where Found

Magnolias develop mostly in the eastern United States, from southern Maine to the tip of Florida, at that point west over the inlet states into eastern Texas.

Strategies For USE

The most restoratively viable piece of the magnolia tree is the bark, which is generally made into a tea. Include two teaspoons of destroyed bark, new or dried, to 16 ounces of boiling water. Stew for 30 minutes, at that point, adds water to make 16 ounces. Strain the tea and take it by the tablespoon varying.

When utilizing magnolia remotely, twofold the measure of bark utilized in the formula.

Milkweed
Asclepias tuberosa

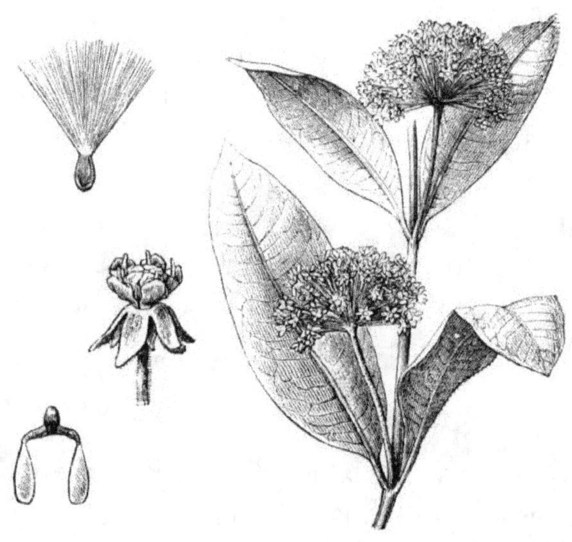

It's been said that the ideal approach to discover milkweed, otherwise called butterfly weed, is to discover a butterfly. That is because butterflies like to lay their eggs among milkweed's brilliant orange flowers.

Native Americans bit crude milkweed pull as a treatment for asthma, bronchitis, typhoid fever, pleurisy, and clog. They additionally utilized a tea, made by baking the seeds in milk, to assuage the runs. A powder produced using the roots was cleaned on wounds to quit dying. When beating into a poultice, the new roots were applied to growing, wounds, and snakebites.

Today, milkweed is most normally utilized as a treatment for moles. The milk-like juice found in the stems contains tissues softening proteins, which are said to destroy these unattractive developments whenever applied every day.

Physical Characteristics

Milkweed is perpetual that grows two to four feet high. It has oval leaves an inch or two long and flowers that might be orange-white or purple, contingent upon the species.

Where Found

Milkweed develops richly all through the United States and Canada. It inclines toward dry, radiant conditions and is regularly found in fields and fields.

Strategies For USE

To make a milkweed tea, bubble four ounces of the new root in three quarts of water until the fluid is decreased to a quart. Strain, let cool and drink varying.

To evacuate moles, break the stems to separate the smooth squeeze and apply it straightforwardly to the mole once per day.

Mullein
Verbascum Thapsus

Mullein is another herb that Native Americans used to treat conditions in every aspect of the body. To treat headache, they would put a mullein poultice on the brow. Numerous clans smoked dried mullein to relieve respiratory conditions, for example, asthma and bronchitis. Mullein likewise was squashed and applied to swellings, hyper-extends, wounds, consumes, and wounds. A germ-free fluid produced using the flowers of the plant was utilized to ease ear infections. In certain districts, Native Americans even put the fluffy leaves of mullein inside their shoes to keep their feet warm.

Specialists have affirmed that mullein is useful for treating respiratory illnesses. As indicated by herbal power Daniel B.

Mowrey, Ph.D., mullein contains significant levels of adhesive and saponins, making it perfect for conditions, for example, hacks, asthma, and even emphysema. Herbalist David Hoffmann concurs, referring to mullein's capacity to diminish irritation while likewise "invigorating liquid creation and along these lines encouraging expectoration."

Mullein likewise shows a guarantee for feed fever sufferers. It seems to restrain the retention of allergens through the mucous layers of the nose. At the point when utilized remotely, the plant has been appeared to have anti-infection and mitigating properties—which clarifies why Native Americans utilized it effectively as a disinfectant for wounds and as a swish for sore throats. The tea produced using the plant may likewise have a quieting impact, as per Dr. Mowrey.

Physical Characteristics

Mullein is a strong biennial with 6-to 15-inch hairy leaves and tall, yellow, blooming stalks.

Where Found

This is a herb that can and grows about anyplace. It very well may be found all through North America in mountains, along roadways, and in all around tended nurseries.

Strategies For USE

Even though mullein flowers are the most restoratively helpful, the leaves and roots likewise have therapeutic forces. For a powerful hack cure and decongestant, herbalist Ana Nez Heatherley prescribes utilizing mullein as a tea. Include an ounce of new, broken mullein leaves to two cups of boiling water. Let steep 10 to 15 minutes, strain, and take varying. A few people add honey to the tea, which improves the taste.

The seeds of the mullein plant are harmful and shouldn't be utilized. Mullein additionally ought not to be utilized in any structure by individuals on anticoagulant medicine or the individuals who are pregnant.

Nettle
Urtica dioica

Here's a herb that was truly a "hit" among Native Americans. To help ease the agonies of joint pain, they would take long twigs and swat the influenced joints, exchanging joint agony for the sting of bother's thorny needles. An instance of taking from one to give to another? Not so much. Research has indicated that the sting delivered by bothering makes the body produce synthetic compounds that have calming and agony lessening powers.

Native Americans didn't simply swing bramble. They heated the base of the plant to make an alleviating salve, and against ligament, poultices were produced using the plant's leaves. A few clans bubbled and ate the plant—admirably; it turns out, because bother has significant levels of boron, a mineral that can help ease joint inflammation.

Presently known to be a phenomenal styptic (a substance fit for halting bloodstream), bother was additionally used to treat genuine injuries. Now and again, wounds were tidied with powder produced using dried nettle or wrapped with nettle leaves that had been gently beating to discharge their therapeutic juices.

Bother was utilized inside, as well—as a tea to control inward draining and as an expectorant to help clear mucus from the lungs. It was accepted that annoy could reinforce the blood—which, as a result of its significant levels of iron and vitamin C (which enables the body to assimilate iron), it likely did.

Researchers currently accept that nettle tea might be useful regarding conditions as fluctuated as asthma, bladder contaminations, bronchitis, gum ailment, prostate augmentation, premenstrual disorder, kidney stones, bursitis, tendinitis, and conceivably even male pattern baldness.

Physical Characteristics

Nettle is an enduring that takes after mint. It develops to around three feet in tallness and has a prickly stem and marginally "shaggy" spiked edged, heart-formed leaves. It creates little green flowers that sprout from pre-summer through late-summer.

Where Found

Nettle is as strong as it is healthful. It tends to be found in many pieces of North America, regularly developing in spring beds, along fences, and in seepage trench close to roadways. It loves a soggy, semi-obscure condition; however, it can do well anyplace it's transplanted.

Strategies For USE

For inward conditions, nettle is best taken as a tea. Add one to two teaspoons of the herb to some boiling water, let represent 10 minutes, at that point strain and drink varying. For joint inflammation, wear gloves to ensure your hands and softly bat the plant against the influenced territories.

Oak
Quercus robur

Compelling in its own right, the oak tree was utilized by Native Americans to keep them forceful—or possibly healthy—also. The Houmas clan would pulverize the foundations of the tree and blend them in with liquor to alleviate hurting joints. The Ojibwa heated the bark as looseness of the bowel's cure; different clans utilized oak bark tea as an expectorant, some pre-owned douches made no sweat the agony and tingling of hemorrhoids. Indeed, even the oak seeds were being used because they invigorated thirst, as Native Americans perceived the health advantages of drinking a lot of water.

How powerful medication is oak by the present gauges? Research shows that the bark of the tree contains mixes called tannins, which can eliminate germs and help decrease irritation. Present-day herbalists suggest oak tea for treating sinus clog and postnasal dribble related to colds. This tea is additionally utilized as a rinse for treating sore throats, laryngitis, and aggravated tonsils.

As indicated by herbalist Alma Hutchins, oak tea frees the stomach from the abundance of bodily fluid, which she accepts can enable the body to assimilate increasingly crucial supplements from nourishments.

Physical Characteristics

There are 58 assortments of oak trees, which generally shift in size and perfect developing conditions. Most are described by their large, three-pronged leaves, which produce little flowers in April, trailed by oak seeds not long after.

Where Found

Oaks develop inexhaustibly all through the vast majority of North America. They don't get along admirably at high rises or in regions that are extremely dry or rough.

Strategies For USE

The bark of the oak tree is the place you'll locate the most grounded restorative "chomp." The most noteworthy strength bark is reaped during mid-to pre-summer. To make a tea, include a teaspoonful of new or dried bark to some boiling water. Let represent 10 to 15 minutes, strain, and drink up to three times each day.

Oats
Avena sativa

Most popular today as healthful breakfast nourishment, plentiful in B vitamins, phosphorus, iron, and dietary fiber, oats were once considered as much medication as a supper. Native Americans utilized teas produced using oats to treat loose bowels. Oats were likewise accepted to help calm uneasiness and discouragement. Poultices produced using oats were used to help heal skin conditions, for example, mouth blisters, dermatitis, bubbles, and hives.

Physical Characteristics

Oats develop on straight, three-foot stalks. The most palatable and restoratively valuable piece of the plant is its seeds, which are encased in an extreme, stringy frame.

Where Found
Oats initially developed wild all through North America, however, now they're chiefly designed. The best spot to discover oats is in your market's grain passageway or the mass canisters at health nourishment stores.

Strategies For USE
Even though all pieces of the oat plant are restoratively dynamic, the grain's generally utilized, frequently in skin-relieving showers. In his book The Green Pharmacy, herbal power James A. Duke, Ph.D., prescribes adding a few bunches of cereal to a hot bath to help soothe dry, bothersome skin and to decrease the disturbance of hives.

Oregon Grape
Mohania aquifolium

Even though this plant has accomplished more of late to improve individuals' scenes than their health, its therapeutic forces rank, "among the most remarkable of all Native American herbs," as indicated by herbalists Gaea and Shandor Weiss. Oregon grape was well known among Native Americans of the Northwest and California, who utilized it as a root tea for treating fevers, stomach aches, reduced craving, and liver issues, and as a poultice for infected gums.

As of late, Oregon grape has been utilized to scrub the spleen and help in processing. It's likewise excellent for the skin, as per herbal position David B. Mowrey, Ph.D., creator of The Scientific Validation of Herbal Medicine. "It can re-establish the skin to a smooth, clear condition following any sort of skin sickness or different disease that may have dried out the skin or delivered bruises."

Physical Characteristics

Oregon grape is a quickly developing bush, three to six feet high, with gleaming, dull green leaves that take after those of the holly tree. It has little, yellowish-green flowers, which offer an approach to dark blue, eatable berries that develop in bundles like grapes. The plant's foundations, be that as it may, are its most therapeutic segment.

Where Found

Oregon grape will develop almost anyplace, yet its regular living space is in the western United States, from Colorado to northern California and north into Canada.

Strategies For USE

Oregon grape is best arranged as a tea. Include a large portion of an ounce of dried root to a quart of boiling water and let steep for 10 to 15 minutes. Strain, let cool and drink up to three cups every day. This arrangement can additionally be applied to the skin to treat psoriasis and skin inflammation.

Peppermint
Mentha piperita

Figure mint and you may think julep, or maybe a tablet to improve your breath.

Not so for Native Americans. Mint was one of their most esteemed prescriptions, used to help to process, lessen fever, mitigate stomach pain, calm menstrual spasms, treat colds, stop colic in infants, and increment craving in individuals who were wiped out. Peppermint poultices were thought to decrease growing and calm painful joints. Powders produced using dried peppermint leaves were now and again sniffed, similar to snuff, to treat migraines and improve focus.

Peppermint's ubiquity has just become throughout the hundreds of years, and it's among the most generally utilized herbs around the world. Various medication organizations add peppermint oil to mints to mitigate acid reflux. It's likewise a fixing in topical treatments that facilitate the pain of joint pain.

Menthol, a fixing in peppermint, has been appeared to build the stomach's yield of stomach related juices, which is the reason it's a guide to assimilation. Applied to the skin, it can mitigate intense squeezing and different kinds of restricted pain. Different utilizations for menthol incorporate the treatment of sickness, painful feminine cycle, intestinal gas, spinal pain, emphysema (menthol is a powerful expectorant), gum sickness, gallstones, fever, ear infections, hives, anxiety, sleep deprivation, and, obviously, halitosis (awful breath).

Physical Characteristics
Peppermint, as a rule, arrives at tallness of somewhere in the range of two and four feet. It has violet flowers that develop in whorls and can be recognized from different sorts of mint by its leaves, which are not as "bushy" as other mint assortments and a more deep shade of green.

Where Found
Peppermint is native to Europe and Australia, yet is very settled in the United States and Canada. A reliable enduring, peppermint does best in a wet, semi-obscure condition. You can't develop it from seed since it delivers none; however cuttings are handily transplanted. It's most intense when collected in pre-fall before the stems become woody.

Strategies For USE

Methods for utilizing peppermint are almost as various as the conditions it can treat. Here, as indicated by Rodale's Illustrated Encyclopedia of Herbs, are the absolute generally normal.

For fart: Suck on a sugar cube to which you've included a few drops of peppermint oil.

For stomach pain: Drink some warm milk enhanced with new peppermint leaves.

For a sleeping disorder: Drink some peppermint tea, made by including a teaspoonful of fresh or dried peppermint to some boiling water and permitting it to soak for 10 minutes.

For colds or influenza: Drink some peppermint tea that incorporates a teaspoonful of new or dried chamomile.

For headache: Crush newly assembled peppermint leaves and apply them as a poultice to your temple.

For toothache: Apply a couple of drops of peppermint oil to the irritated tooth.

For dry hands: Wash your hands in peppermint tea.

For sore throat: Gargle with tepid peppermint tea.

For bug nibbles or stings: Crush a new peppermint leaf and apply the poultice.

For terrible breath: Chew on a bunch of fresh peppermint leaves and stems.

Pine
Pinus

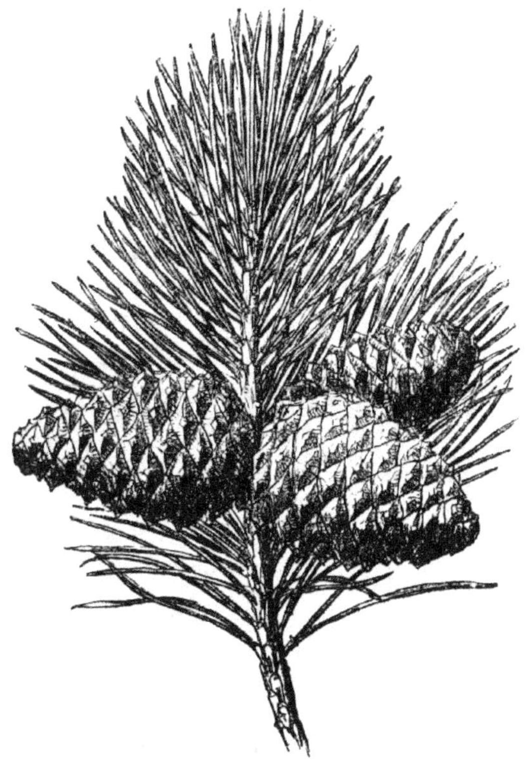

For Americans today, the pine tree is seen primarily as an image of Christmas cheer—however, pine was one of the Native Americans' most significant prescriptions. They made biting gum from pine pitch, which they discovered relieving for sore throats. Pine needles were squashed and built into the glue for a sweet-smelling cerebral pain poultice. The bark was likewise utilized as a poultice for such things as wounds, consumes, ulcers, and hemorrhoids. Balms produced using pine gums were used to treat sore muscles and joints, and pine tea was a well-known solution for colds, hacks, and upper respiratory clog.

Now and again, the needles were touched off because Native Americans accepted that breathing pine vapor could calm spinal pain.

Herbalists keep on suggesting pine cures, frequently for treating upper respiratory issues. Teas produced using dried needles might be valuable for facilitating joint pain, and pine showers may help decrease skin disturbance just as tension.

Physical Characteristics

There are more than 90 assortments of pine trees, yet all can be categorized as one of two classifications: yellow pine and delicate white pine, which is the more therapeutically dynamic of the two. White pine is portrayed by its more extended, milder needles, all the more awkward branches, and a bushier, less triangular shape.

Where Found

Thirty types of pine trees are native to North America and can be found in many pieces of the landmass.

Strategies For USE

To cause a pine tea, pour some boiling water onto a large portion of a teaspoonful of dried needles and young buds, which are best gathered in the spring. Let represent 10 to 15 minutes, strain, and drink varying, for the most part, up to three times each day. To utilize pine as an inhalant, put a few bunches of new needles, buds, and twigs in an enormous pot, spread with water, and heat to the point of boiling. Lessen the warmth and stew for five minutes. Expel from heat, at that point, breathe in the steam for 15 minutes by hanging over the pot, utilizing a towel over your head to trap the steam.

For an unwinding, skin-accommodating shower, splash three bunches of new pine twigs in around two pints of water for 30 minutes. At that point, heat the blend to the end of boiling and

stew for 10 minutes. Strain the fluid and add it to your
bathwater.

Purslane
Portulaca

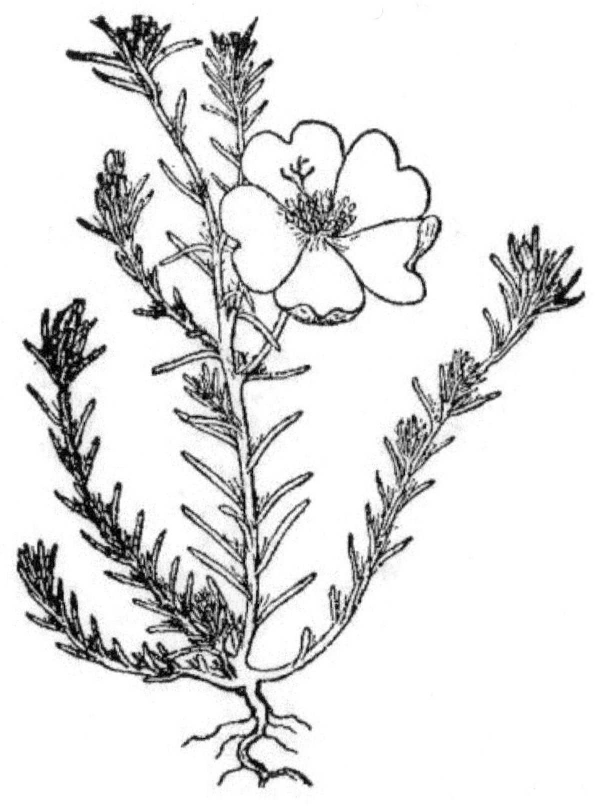

Purslane is one of those herbs that is as significant as a vegetable for what it's worth as a medication. Eaten cooked or crude, purslane is a fantastic wellspring of the cell reinforcement vitamins A, C, and E. It likewise contains riboflavin, calcium, phosphorus, magnesium, and iron. Purslane additionally is the most extravagant realized plant wellspring of omega-3 unsaturated fats. These unsaturated fats, which are primarily found in fish oils, may help decrease the danger of coronary illness by bringing down cholesterol and circulatory strain and by lessening the propensity of the blood to shape clusters in the veins. Research has likewise indicated that omega-3 unsaturated fats may support resistance and help facilitate the agony of joint pain.

Since purslane contains inexhaustible measures of magnesium, it's occasionally suggested for fighting ceaseless weakness and migraines. It additionally contains lithium, a temperament balancing out intensify that can help ease wretchedness.

Native Americans most likely ate purslane, yet they were increasingly intrigued by its therapeutic applications. Juice from the plant's leaves was found to mitigate consumes, creepy crawly chomps and stings, and ear infections. A tea produced using the leaves was thought to calm looseness of the bowels, stomach ache, and urinary tract contaminations—and because purslane contains a great deal of vitamin C, it could be utilized to treat and forestall scurvy.

Herbalists today here and there suggest purslane for its healing properties. It's a fantastic skin chemical and astringent (skin tightener) and might be useful in treating skin inflammation and wrinkles.

Physical Characteristics

Purslane develops as a thick, tangle like ground spread around eight inches high. Its oval-formed leaves, roughly one inch long, are thick and shiny, and are joined by little, splendid yellow flowers that sprout from June through September.

Where Found

Purslane develops almost wherever in North America. Indeed, it's regularly seen as an annoyance weed in vegetable and flower gardens. It additionally can be produced from seed in six to about two months in all around depleted soil that gets a lot of suns.

Strategies For USE

The leaves, stems, and flowers of purslane can be eaten crude as serving of mixed greens fixings, or steamed or bubbled as a vegetable comparable in taste to asparagus. The plant's seeds can be ground and added to flour or different nourishments as a dietary lift.

For therapeutic use, the leaves can be broken, and their juice applied straightforwardly to consumes or creepy crawly nibbles and stings. To utilize purslane inside, heat the whole plant for 15 to 20 minutes. Strain the water, let cool, and drink as a tea. A few herbalists prescribe this solution for alleviating stomach pain, looseness of the bowels, and agonizing pee, even though in instances of bladder disease, don't neglect your primary care physician's recommendation, which may incorporate a medicine for anti-infection agents. Purslane can likewise be utilized as a diuretic to help free the assortment of abundant water.

As a skin help, purslane has the upside of being much less expensive than fancier business arrangements. To set up a skin chemical and astringent, place a cup of hacked purslane leaves and stems between two bits of double-layered cheesecloth. Put the pack in a bowl and squash altogether with a potato masher or pestle. When the herb has been all around squashed, include some lukewarm water to the pot and keep crushing the purslane until all the juices have been separated.

Apply the blend to your face and leave it on for around five minutes, at that point flush altogether. Purslane will clean, fix, and revive the skin, and can assist smooth with fine lines and shallow wrinkles.

The planning will keep for as long as five days, as long as you store it in the fridge in a firmly fixed holder.

Sassafras
Sassafras albidum

Hardly any plants were viewed as profoundly or utilized as broadly by Native Americans as the sassafras tree. When European pioneers showed up and saw what sassafras could do, updates on this energizing plant immediately headed out back to Europe. "This tree at one time made more noteworthy enthusiasm for the Old World than some other American item, not aside from tobacco," composed antiquarian John Lloyd. Legend recommends that America probably won't have been found by the Europeans at all had it not been for this sweet-smelling tree. Christopher Columbus is said to have been made aware of the nearness of land by the sweet smell of the late-winter leaves of the sassafras tree.

Native Americans utilized sassafras roots to make poultices for wounds and skin contaminations. Both the roots and berries were broadly used to make teas for treating queasiness, fevers, weakness, gas pains, menstrual agony, red heat, and even syphilis. Utilized remotely, a decoction produced using sassafras root has been demonstrated to be a useful disinfectant. Numerous herbalists prescribe this decoction to ease poison ivy rashes and to slaughter lice. A readiness produced using the sticky center of sassafras branches was utilized by Native Americans to alleviate tired eyes.

Physical Characteristics

By and large 30 to 50 feet tall, sassafras is a deciduous tree with little, exceptionally sweet-smelling, glove molded leaves that may have a couple of "thumbs." It has a dark, profoundly furrowed bark and a thick trunk that can arrive at six feet in the distance across. It bears little, greenish-yellow flowers in the spring.

Where Found

Sassafras is found in many pieces of the eastern United States, stretching out as far west as Michigan and Texas.

Strategies For USE

To diminish rashes or purify shallow cuts or scratches, include two ounces of new sassafras leaves to 16 ounces of boiling water and let stew for 15 minutes to 60 minutes. After the blend has cooled, apply it to the influenced territories as a wet pack.

Squaw Weed
Senecio aureus

As the name proposes, squaw weed, additionally called "life root," was utilized basically to treat issues experienced by Native American ladies. The Catawba of the Southeast, for instance, used a squaw weed tea to facilitate the agony of labor and to soothe manifestations of the troublesome period. The herb was utilized by different clans to stop inward draining and was likewise thought to be an energizer.

As indicated by herbalist David Hoffmann, squaw weed was at times utilized as a douche to treat leukorrhea, a condition that causes unreasonable vaginal bodily fluid.

Physical Characteristics

Squaw weed is a little enduring, somewhere in the range of one and two feet high, with an erect, smooth stem. Adjusted leaves develop scantily at the base area of the plant, and fluffy greenery like leaves grow from the top segment. It bears little yellow flowers during May and June.

- **Where Found**

Squaw weed develops principally in the eastern United States. It inclines toward wet regions, for example, swamps and the banks of streams and rivers.

Strategies For USE

Squaw weed is best taken as a tea, utilizing a teaspoonful of dried herb (root or leaves) in some boiling water. Permit the tea to soak 10 to 15 minutes, strain, and drink three to four times each day.

Caution: Don't drink squaw weed tea multiple times each day since it very well may be lethal in huge sums.

Valerian

Valeriana officianalis

This plant may have been among the world's absolute first sedatives. Its name gets from the Latin word *valere*, which signifies "boldness"— a quality that may have been cultivated by the herb's capacity to lessen uneasiness and dread. Numerous individuals in England tasted valerian tea to consistent their nerves during the German air bombardments of World War II.

Native Americans were very much aware of valerian's loosening up impacts—on the body just like the brain. The roots were eaten either dried or crude to treat solid squeezing, intestinal colic, and the pains of the monthly cycle. A few clans ground valerian's carrot-like roots into a flour, which they blended into bread or mush.

Valerian is one of the most broadly utilized herbs on the planet today. Herbalists suggest it for uneasiness, a sleeping disorder, headache migraines, cerebral strain pains, hypertension, irregular heartbeat, hives, upset absorption, and hyperactivity in youngsters. It additionally may help soothe joint pain in those situations where the condition is exacerbated by pressure.

Physical Characteristics
Valerian is an enduring herb that usually develops to be two to five feet in stature. It has a light green stem, enormous leaves, and bright yellow flowers that sprout from June through August. Its underlying foundations, which contain a large portion of the therapeutic mixes, have a smell that has been contrasted with dirty socks.

Where Found
Valerian is native to Europe and western Asia, yet now is additionally found in the northern United States and Canada. It favors sodden territories, for example, woods, low-lying mountains, and the banks of waterways and streams.

Strategies For USE
Valerian is best taken as a root tea, made by adding one to two teaspoons of dried herb to some boiling water. Let it steep 10 to 15 minutes; at that point, strain and drink varying.
Felines are unequivocally pulled in to the fragrance of valerian, so don't be shocked if your feline attempts to plunge his hairs into your cup. Make sure to store the herb very much fixed.
Lamentably, rodents are likewise pulled in by the smell. It's been recommended that it wasn't the flute-playing of the amazing Pied Piper that tricked rodents to their demises; however, the smell of the valerian he stuffed in his pockets!

Violet

Viola

Esteemed for more than its pretty face, the wild violet turned into a therapeutic backbone for some Native American clans. The Ojibwa are accounted for to have utilized a decoction produced using the underlying foundations of the white violet for treating bladder pain and one using the foundations of the yellow violet for sore throats. The Potawatomi utilized the underlying foundations of the yellow violet as a tonic for heart issues. Different clans used different types of violet for looseness of the bowels, fever, gas, heartburn, bronchitis, migraines, and reduced flow.

Researchers have discovered that most types of violet, notwithstanding being incredible wellsprings of vitamins A and C, contain a substance like the dynamic fixing in headache medicine.

Violets likewise are wealthy in a substance called rutin, which research shows can fortify hairlike dividers, potentially making it supportive for forestalling and treating varicose veins. The examinations indicated that rutin is powerful in sums running from 20 to 100 milligrams. A half-cup of new violet flowers contains somewhere in the range of 200 and 2,300 milligrams of rutin, says herbal power James A. Duke, Ph.D.

Physical Characteristics

There are more than 400 types of wild violet. Most are perennials, yet some develop every year. They buy and extensive arrive at four to six crawls in tallness, have oval leaves, and little white, violet, or yellow flowers that sprout in April and May.

Where Found

Violet can be found all through the United States. It inclines toward soggy, obscure conditions, and frequently develops close to tall greenery and inside scanty forests.

Strategies For USE

All pieces of the violet are restoratively dynamic and can be utilized new or dried. Make a tea by baking any portion of the plant for around 15 minutes, using a teaspoonful of the herb in some water. Or on the other hand, you can cause the tea into a syrup with further boiling to decrease the fluid and including a tad of honey.

Native Americans, some of the time, utilized violet poultices, which they applied to the head as a treatment for migraines.

The African violet isn't identified with wild violet and ought not to be utilized as medication.

Watercress
Nasturtium officinale

If you, as of now, appreciate the fiery chomp of watercress in sandwiches and plates of mixed greens, you should take an additional aiding for your health. Watercress is extraordinarily nutritious, with restorative measures of vitamins A, C, and E, alongside minerals, for example, calcium, magnesium, iron, and copper. Albeit native to Europe, it didn't take long to spread all through North America and Mexico, and Native Americans immediately found its healing forces.

They utilized watercress tea to treat liver and kidney issues, gallstones, apprehension, colds, and an assortment of upper respiratory diseases. Juice from the plant's leaves was utilized remotely to treat skin conditions, for example, skin inflammation and ringworm. The extract was even applied to the scalp trying to forestall male pattern baldness.

Physical Characteristics

Watercress is portrayed by green stems one to three feet in length. It has little white flowers and beefy elliptical leaves that develop in bunch of three to seven leaves each.

Where Found

Watercress develops all through the United States and Mexico and the more significant part of Canada. Search for it developing in shallow rivers, along with the edges of moderate moving waterways, and in lakes and lakes, any place the water is clean, fresh, and running. The herb does best in water two to six inches down. Its green stems, for the most part, distend a few crawls over the water's surface. It's additionally generally accessible in grocery stores.

Strategies For USE

To make watercress tea, include a teaspoonful of dried or new herb to some boiling water. Let represent around 10 minutes; at that point, strain and drink varying. A similar tea can likewise be utilized as a skin wash for rashes, dermatitis, or skin break out.

For a progressively astringent facial tonic, pound the leaves to extricate the juice and apply it to your skin. A few herbalists suggest blending watercress squeeze in with a little vinegar and using it to the temple to get a brisk shock of vitality.

Wild watercress ought to be altogether washed because it might harbor parasites. In enormous sums, it might aggravate the kidneys, so you would prefer not to utilize it consistently.

White Poplar
Populus tremuloides

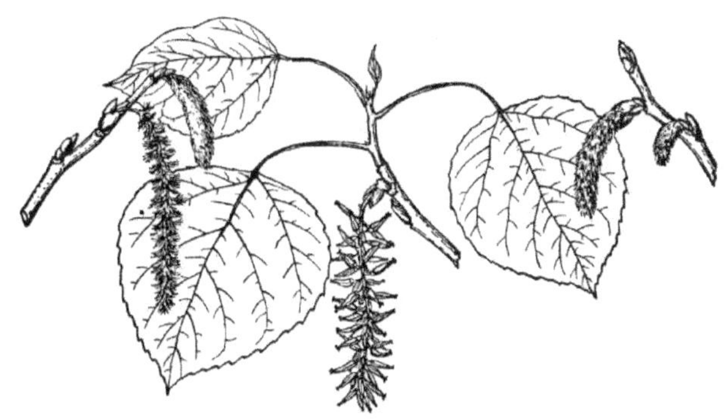

Although the soonest pioneers esteemed poplar for the most part as wood for making furniture, Native Americans prized the tree as medication. They utilized poplar for conditions as differed as colds, fever, and looseness of the bowels, joint inflammation, urinary tract contaminations, general shortcoming, and loss of craving. All the more significantly, they utilized poplar to treat broken bones, using a strategy that stunned early pilgrims.

A fluid produced using baking up the tree's husk was cooled, at that point, poured over the harmed region to diminish pain. At that point, a healer would set the messed up bone, so all things considered, a cast was produced using poplar wood to balance out the break. Early pilgrims are said to have wondered about the achievement of this system, which far outperformed their medications.

Science has affirmed that Native Americans were flawless. Poplar contains mixes artificially like the ingredients in headache medicine. Poplar cures decreased pain and irritation, which could support genuine wounds, for example, broken bones, heal all the more rapidly.

Physical Characteristics

Poplar is a deciduous tree, 40 to 50 feet tall, with a light dim bark and dull green, heart-formed leaves that turn brilliant yellow in the fall.

Where Found

It's challenging to think about a spot where poplar trees don't develop. They're found all through the United States and Canada, in atmosphere zones extending from subtropical to subarctic.

Strategies For USE

It no longer bodes well to utilize poplar for treating broken bones, since your primary care physician will do a superior, and more secure, work. Nonetheless, you can use poplar tea to diminish the pain of joint pain. Add one to two teaspoons of new or dried poplar bark, which is best when it's gathered in the spring, to some boiling water. Diminish the warmth and let stew for 15 minutes. Strain the fluid, let cool, and drink up to three times each day, or all the more regularly to control pain.

Willow
Salix

The rundown of ills for which Native American healers utilized the willow tree appears to be sufficiently long to fill a clinical word reference. Clans in California utilized a willow bark tea for treating back pain. The Pima of Arizona utilized a decoction produced using willow leaves to lessen fever.

The Menominee of the Midwest made a root tea for treating colic and looseness of the bowels. The Montagnais of eastern Canada utilized a mush produced using the bark to ease cerebral pain. The rundown continues endlessly.

There's not, at this point, any uncertainty that willow entirely merits its healing notoriety. It's a rich wellspring of a compound called salicin, which is fundamentally the same as the pain executing, fever-decreasing fixing in anti-inflammatory medicine.

In his book The Green Pharmacy, herbal position James A. Duke, Ph.D., distinguishes 23 conditions for which willow has demonstrated advantageous, not the least of which is a coronary illness. Research has indicated that taking between one-half and one tablet of conventional headache medicine a day can considerably lessen the danger of ischemic episodes and strokes. Anti-inflammatory medication represses the arrangement of blood clusters that can square corridors and keep blood from arriving at the heart or mind. It's conceivable to get the equivalent defensive impacts by drinking one cup of willow bark tea each other day, he says.

Willow tea gives off an impression of being useful in any condition ordinarily treated by anti-inflammatory medicine, as per Dr. Duke. The rundown incorporates osteoarthritis, back pain, bursitis, tendinitis, migraine, ear infection, toothache, carpal passage disorder, colds, and fever.

Willow bark tea isn't high, Dr. Duke notes. On the off chance that headache medicine bothers your stomach, willow bark may do likewise. In any case, you might have the option to lessen uneasiness by including a teaspoonful of dried licorice root to the willow before you begin blending the tea.

Willow can likewise be utilized remotely. Native American healers used the bark to break down corns and callused bunions. A poultice made with dried willow root powder can also ease corns. A few herbalists suggest utilizing a robust willow tea as a wash for sore throats, just as a disinfectant for shallow cuts and scratches.

The acids in willow can be bothering, nonetheless, so it's imperative to keep the fluid off the encompassing skin, however much as could reasonably be expected.

Physical Characteristics

There are roughly 300 types of willow, extending in size from modest hedges, not precisely an inch high to trees overshadowing 100 feet. The most significant and most basic assortment in North America is the dark willow, which is recognized by its profoundly furrowed, dark earthy colored bark, ruddy to orange twig-like branches, and long, thin leaves that decrease to a point.

Where Found

Willow develops nearly as promptly as it heals. It's found in many pieces of North America, the particular case being the northern-most areas of Canada. It will develop so vivaciously under wet conditions that it can generally be begun in soggy territories from a cutting.

Strategies For USE

To make willow tea, include a teaspoonful of dried bark to some boiling water, let steep for 15 minutes, at that point strain and drink varying.

Caution: Because willow bark contains mixes like those in headache medicine, it ought not to be given to kids as it might build the danger of Reye's disorder, a conceivably genuine neurological issue.

Wormwood
Artemisia absinthium

As its name recommends, wormwood—additionally called sagebrush—was utilized frequently by Native Americans to cleanse parasites from the intestinal tract. They drank hot wormwood tea for fever, acid reflux, queasiness, and agonizing monthly cycle. They applied poultices of wormwood leaves to assuage the pain of joint inflammation, and the leaves likewise were dried, powdered, and tidied on babies experiencing diaper rash. At the point when arranged as a salve, wormwood was likewise used to repulse bugs and to clean injuries.

Wormwood is frequently applied remotely to treat difficult wounds and injuries. As indicated by herbalist John Lust, "The herb goes about as a neighborhood sedative and can be helpful in calming the agonies of ailment, neuralgia (nerve pain) and joint inflammation."

As increasingly confirmation that Native Americans were dynamic in healing, the makers of Absorbine Jr. remember concentrates of wormwood among the dynamic elements for this over-the-counter liniment for muscle and back agony

.

Physical Characteristics

Wormwood is a tall, thick plant comparative in appearance and fragrance to sage. It develops to somewhere in the range of two and four feet high, with leaves around four inches in length and little yellow flowers dissipated all through the shrub. The flowers sprout from June through September.

Where Found

Wormwood develops for the most part as a weed in the western and northern United States and furthermore in southern Canada.

Strategies For USE

You can make a wormwood tea by including a teaspoonful of squashed leaves (dried or new) to one cup of boiling water and soaking for around 15 minutes. Drink the tea as a mellow calming, stomach related guide, or cold cure, or use it remotely as a germ-free for cuts and scratches, or as a gentle topical sedative for relieving hyper-extends, sore muscles, or joint agony.

Wormwood shouldn't be utilized during pregnancy or by anybody experiencing bronchitis or emphysema. A few people are sensitive to wormwood; if a rash creates, quit utilizing it right away.

Yarrow
Achillea millefolium

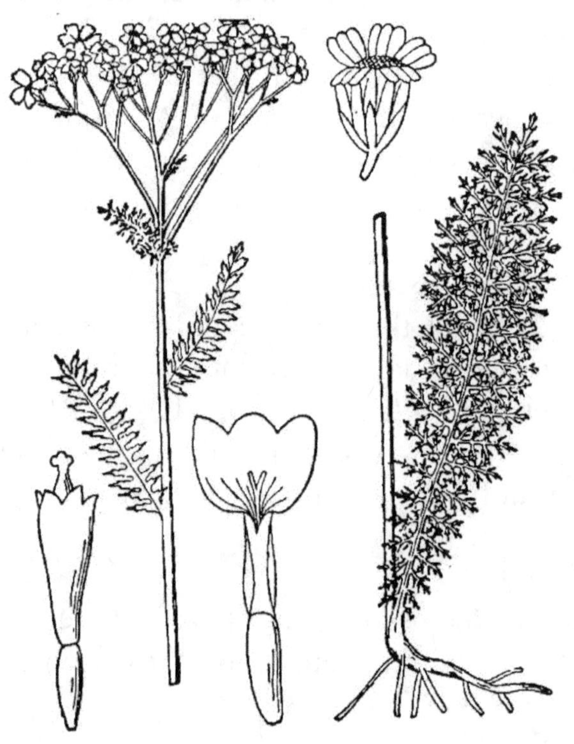

The restorative history of this herb is the length of the rundown of ills it can treat. The Greek saint Achilles is said to have utilized yarrow to treat the injuries of his stricken warriors. Native Americans likewise utilized yarrow for wounds, yet that was only the start.

Yarrow was frequently taken as a tea for stomach issues and fever. It was made into poultices for treating rashes, expanding, dermatitis, and bug nibbles. Students of history gauge that 46 unique clans use yarrow for upwards of 28 issues, making it one of the most broadly utilized herbs.

Present-day herbalists have made the rundown much more. Some suggest yarrow for hypertension, ulcers, interior and outer dying, liver issues, loose bowels, colds and influenza, bad-tempered bowel syndrome, Crohn's ailment, bladder contaminations, gas pains, hemorrhoids, overwhelming menstrual stream, and issues related with menopause. It additionally goes about as a gentle narcotic and can help ease nervousness and a sleeping disorder. A juice produced using the leaves can help decrease the redness of ragged looking eyes.

Physical Characteristics

Yarrow develops to around three feet in tallness. It has fluffy leaves and shelter of white or pink flowers at the top. It has an enjoyably sweet fragrance, yet a severe taste because of its high therapeutic substance.

Where Found

Yarrow develops all through the United States and the majority of Canada, normally in glades, pastures, and alongside the road. It develops well when developed, and can endure for all intents and purposes any dirt that is not very wet or vigorously concealed.

Strategies For USE

The most intense pieces of the plant are the highest leaves and flowers, which are appropriate for making tea. A few herbalists prescribe making a poultice and applying yarrow straightforwardly to the skin. At times, it's even a bit to calm toothache.

To make a tea, add one to two teaspoons of leaves or flowers (dried or new) to some boiling water. Let represent 15 minutes, strain, and drink varying—or you can apply the tea to the skin to ease consumes, wounds, or different disturbances.

CHAPTER 3 - DIY Herbal Recipes

Some special homemade herbs, their restorative benefits, ingredients and how to make.

Elder

Sambucus spp.
Adoxaceae family

Elder Bushes appear to spring up wherever in fields, glades, and rural yards. This liberal plant is spread by winged creatures and creatures eating the berries and scattering the seeds. Unassuming, fragile, foamy bloom heads in spring and late-spring are trailed by gem-like garnet to dark berries. A sensitive flower aroma drifts on the breeze. Elder was gone before just by chamomile when I initially set going to discover valuable wild plants, so elder and I go route back. It would be unimaginable currently to confront winter without a decent stockpile of senior's abundance.

Elder has been a stunning partner to mankind from before recorded time, yet there is an immense and clashing legend related to the plant. Contingent upon who does the telling, the elder plant is considered either defensive or risky. For example, elder can shield one from witches or the wood can turn into an enchantment wand. Different sources clarify that the wood repulses lightning, while others state that it draws lightning. Almost all old compositions believe the plant to be female and propose that you approach the old woman inside for authorization before collecting. Parts of elder wood have for quite some time been utilized for woodwinds and comparative instruments in light of the fact that the external bark encloses a delicate pointed focus that is effortlessly emptied.

Elderberries and elderflowers have been utilized restoratively for colds and influenza for some ages.
Some early recorded occurrences of the berries date to old Greece. A few herbalists like to utilize the flowers, while others depend on the berries, yet in any case, this plant offers us extraordinary advantages. In the eastern United States, the S. Canadensis assortment is the wild bramble found in knolls and forests, while on the West Coast, the wild berries are covered with a light blue fine become flushed. That assortment is S. cerulean (now and then otherwise called S. Mexicana). There are numerous cultivars. The entireties of the purple-dark berried assortments are considered to have comparable properties. Around the globe, there are different customary

dishes and drinks dependent on both the elderflower and the elderberry.

Elderberries can be found in parts of Europe, Asia, South America, and a large portion of the Northern Hemisphere, with numerous assortments being spoken to, contingent upon the area.

In the spring, the flowers show up on huge level umbels up to 15 inches (38 cm) in distance across. The flowers are assembled when they are full and pale cream shaded. Whenever left to create natural product, the berries show up in late-summer fit to be reaped when they are dull and about dark in shading. High in vitamin C, the flowers soaks into a tea are calming, antiviral, and anticatarrhal, and prompt sweat, assisting with hustling an infection on its way. They fill in as a potassium-saving diuretic, freeing tissues and mucous layers from abundance liquid. Notwithstanding interior use, elderflowers love the skin. A solid elderflower water mixture on a pack is said to help spots, age spots, and darkish patches of skin. Verifiably, it was additionally applied generously to lift the warmth of burn from the sun, rosacea, bubbles, and carbuncles. Alleviating and healing to the skin, elderflower is utilized in creams, facials, and facial steams and spa medications.

Elderberries are packed with acceptable stuff! There are numerous bioflavonoids, including very amazing cell reinforcement anthocyanins that make an aloof situation for the replication of infections. At the point when an infection can't repeat, it rapidly washes from the body. Flavonoids (the blue and purple colors) have antibacterial, antiviral, antitumor, mitigating, antiallergenic, and vasodilatory consequences for the body. Numerous individuals discover alleviation inside long periods of taking elderberry groundwork for influenza side effects. Whenever taken at regular intervals for a couple of days, it can totally clear out an obstinate infection. Research has been led on elderberry's impact on influenza with incredible outcomes, and many state organizations presently support the proliferation of elderberry as a yield. Hundreds of years of exact proof have likewise demonstrated this to be valid, however a little controlled research never stings. The business readiness Sambucol has for some time been utilized for quite a long time by the Israeli Air Force when it is important to rapidly recoup from cold or influenza.

The therapeutic segments have been seen as warmth safe, and hence ready to be cooked, making them simple to consolidate into an everyday "nourishment as medication" routine throughout the winter months.

The seeds contain limited quantities of a glycoside, which utilizes into cyanide (as do many organic product seeds), and cooking the berries actuates the therapeutic properties and discharges the unfortunate cyanide build up. Eating in excess of a little bunch of crude berries may cause gastric miracle in certain individuals.

It is extremely simple to develop elderberry. Branches lie over the ground and root, or they can even be established in water. The shrubby hedges will develop in incomplete shade, however are considerably more joyful in full sun. They like loads of water yet will thrive in drier settings if there's a lot of downpour. When set up, they will withstand a great deal of disregard, being a weed all things considered.

There are a couple of nuisances that will cut into the gather. Tent caterpillars must be looked for and evacuated from the outset locating. Winged animals love the berries, and if there isn't sufficient other wild nourishment accessible, they'll eat them all. Natural product flies can likewise assault the berries; however a natural pesticide containing Spinosad and vinegar traps may deal with the issue.

There are such huge numbers of approaches to utilize the flowers and berries. My preferred readiness is to just freeze the berries in 1-quart (1 L) packs with the goal that they are prepared for anything throughout the winter. Both the berries and the flowers are handily dried for sometime in the future.

Restorative Benefits
- Treats cold and influenza
- Promotes pee
- Soothes and heals skin
- Kills infections
- Promotes perspiring
- Reduces aggravation of the aviation routes

Elderberry Juice

The juice can be solidified or canned. Freeze it in 1-cup (235 ml) parcels in a level compartment, enormous enough that the thickened juice is under 1/2-inch (1.3 cm) thick.
It is so natural to sever a piece when required simply.

Ingredients

- 1 quart new elderberries or 1 cup (150 g) dried
- 1 quart (940 ml) water (if utilizing dried berries), in addition to water to cover Directions

Yield: 3 cups (705 ml)

Instructions

Spot the new flushed berries into a dish and add only enough water to abstain from burning. Warmth to a stew and tangle to help discharge the juice as the heat begins to pop the berries. A potato masher is extraordinary for this reason. Proceed with tenderly warming and sometimes crushing until the majority of the berries have blasted and gone to juice. Pour through a fine-work strainer to catch the seeds, or line a filter with a bit of cheesecloth.

This is a genuinely focused juice, and 1 cup (235 ml) taken in 1-tablespoon (15 ml) divides four times each day for three days is sufficient to get an individual through a viral danger.

In the case of utilizing dried berries, absorb the berries 4 cups (940 ml) water expedite and continue as above.

Elderberry Extract/Tincture

This is one of only a handful barely any tinctures that you can make quarts (liters) of every year, and you'll likely either use it yourself or offer it with loved ones. When you perceive how rapidly it can leave an infection speechless, you'll be contributing to everybody, you know.

Ingredients

- Dried or fresh elderberries
- Menstruum (vodka or liquor of decision) to cover

Yield: 1 16 ounces (470 ml)

Instructions

In the case of utilizing dried material, fill a 1-16 ounces (470 ml) container 33% full before including fluid (menstruum is the specific term for the dissolvable or transporter utilized in a concentrate, tincture, or remedy). In the case of using new herbs, fill free to the top.

Elderberry Syrup

This syrup is so tasty it very well may be utilized to improve tea or spread on toast and hotcakes, and the children could reveal to you the subsequent they feel the minor piece scratchy in the throat.

Ingredients

- 1 cup (150 g) dried elderberries or 3 cups (450 g) new or solidified Zest and squeeze from 1 lemon
- 2-to 3-inch (5 to 7.5 cm) bit of ginger root, ground 6-inch (15 cm) bit of cinnamon bark, broken
- Five cardamom cases
- 1 vanilla bean or 1 teaspoon vanilla concentrate
- 3 cups (705 ml) water if utilizing dried berries or 1 cup (235 ml) if using new or solidified 11/2 cups (160 g) honey

Yield: 3 cups (705 ml)

Instructions

Put all the ingredients aside from the honey into a pot and heat to the point of boiling over medium warmth. Lower the warmth, and gradually stew for 30 minutes. Permit to cool, and afterward strain, crushing all the high fluid from the solids. Measure and return the imbuement to a stew until there is 11/2 cups (355 ml) fluid. Permit to cool somewhat and mix in the honey until it is very much fused.

Sugar can be utilized rather than honey. To do that, measure the fluid in the wake of cooking and include twice as much sugar as there is fluid. For instance, if there is 1 cup (235 ml) of fluid, utilize 2 cups (400 g) of sugar. Mix to break down the sugar and afterward heat to the point of boiling for 3 to 5 minutes to lessen somewhat. The measure of sugar or honey is vital as an additive, so if you decide to utilize less, it must be refrigerated and used inside a month or two.

The more significant part of the flavors in the formula can be treated as discretionary (aside from ginger, I love that warming ginger in there), and I at first began adding them to the recipe for the flavor. It was a charming shock to learn years after the fact that cardamom, a seed that is regularly utilized in Indian dishes, has antiviral properties, as well!

Refrigerate for longer stock.

Eldertea Blend

This is an extraordinary mix for kicking that bug before it gets a dependable balance.

Ingredients
One tablespoon dried elderberries
One tablespoon dried elderflowers
1 tablespoon minced solidified ginger
1 tablespoon dried peppermint (substitute half or all with blessed basil if accessible)

Yield: 1/4 cup, enough for 10 to 12 cups of tea

Instructions
Join the herbs in a container and blend well. Utilize an adjusted teaspoonful of the mix per 1 cup (235 ml) of boiling water and steep for at any rate 5 minutes. Include honey and a lemon cut, pull on warm socks, and unwind.

Elderberry Pie

This is a heavenly, delicious berry pie for whenever, however, if there's an infection going around, it's only one all the more method to get a portion of elderberry anticipation.

Ingredients
Cake for a 9-inch (23 cm) two-outside layer pie
3 cups (450 g) elderberries
1/4 teaspoon salt
11/8 cups (225 g) sugar
33/4 tablespoons (56 ml) lemon juice
21/4 tablespoons 18 g) cornstarch
2 tablespoons (28 g) unsalted margarine

Yield: 8 servings

Instructions
Preheat the grill to 425°F (220°C, or gas mark 7). Line a 9-inch (23 cm) pie dish with one of the outsides.
Join the elderberries, salt, sugar, lemon juice, and cornstarch in a pot over medium warmth and cook until thick. Fill the cake lined pie dish. Spot with the margarine. Spread with the top hull. Seal and woodwind. Prick the covering with a fork.
Prepare for 10 minutes; at that point, bring down the broiler temperature to 350°F (180°C, or gas mark 4) and heat for 30 additional minutes, or until the covering is brilliant earthy colored and the juices are bubbly and thickened.

Elderberry Apple Fruit Leather

I make new apple and pear sauce from the trees here on the ranch. Business fruit purée functions admirably as well, however on the off chance that it has a great deal of fluid, strain it out other users.

Ingredients
- 1 cup (235 ml) elderberry juice
- 2 cups (490 g) apple or pear sauce

Yield: 12 × 18-inch (30.5 × 45.7 cm) sheet, cut into segments of your decision

Instructions
Preheat the grill to its most minimal setting. Line a 12 × 18-inch (30.5 × 45.7 cm) rimmed baking sheet with material paper.
Join the juice and fruit purée and mix to mix well. Spread the blend daintily and equitably on the readied baking sheet. Spot in the stove and leave it for a few hours, until it is scarcely cheap to the touch and strips from the material without any problem. You can do this at night and leave it short-term on the off chance that you wish.
Cut the cowhide into strips and wind it around the waxed paper to store for some time in the future. Refrigerate or freeze, except if it is to be utilized inside a couple of days. You can freeze it, so it is prepared for use in winter.

Elderberry Liqueur

Mixers are relatives of natural meds, made as ahead of schedule as the thirteenth century. Early therapeutic legend has them impractically blended by Italian priests in the unspoiled, peaceful open country. You can make alcohol with vodka, yet I like to utilize cognac, which is refined wine, matured in barrels. It's not as cruel as grain liquor or vodka, and when warmed has a rich sweet-smelling aroma. Elderberry wine is known as a tonic to be taken normally to help the resistance. Elderberry alcohol can be tasted like a sweet nightcap for tonic purposes and warmed it takes on an extra job, opening bronchial and sinus entries, giving alleviating solace to an irritated throat, and calming chest clog.

Ingredients

- 2 cups new elderberries or 1 cup dried
- 1 quart (1 L) liquor (if utilizing dried, include 1 cup [235 ml] for splashing) 3 or 4 segments of citrus skin (substance expelled)
- 1 cup (360 g) honey, or to taste

Yield: 1 quart (1 L)

Instructions

In the case of utilizing dried elderberries, place in a bowl, spread with liquor, and splash for the time being. Include the berries (don't strain off the dousing cognac), liquor, and citrus (lemon is my top choice) skin to a moderate cooker.

Spread. Utilizing a sweets thermometer, keep the blend at 145° to 150°F (63° to 65.5°C) for 3 to 5 hours. Be extremely mindful so as not to overheat. If your moderate cooker has at a higher fever on low, abbreviate the implantation time. Cool, strain, and tenderly press through a muslin material. Add honey to taste.

Mix well and fill a disinfected holder. Store in a cool, dull place or refrigerate.

Alternative

Your creative mind and individual taste are as far as possible for added substances. A portion of my top picks to add to the imbuement stage are cinnamon sticks, entire cloves, coarsely hacked nutmeg, turmeric, cardamom, hawthorn berries, juniper berries, raspberries, hibiscus flowers, feverfew, lavender, rosemary, sage, fennel seed, melissa, and thyme.

Passionflower

Passiflora spp.
Passifloraceae family

Passionflower's very unusual flowers don't appear to conceivably be genuine. The short stems on the bloom itself don't loan themselves well to cut flower courses of action, so you would never consider them to be such. At my home, I can't avoid bringing them inside. In the wake of pursuing endlessly any of the ants that adoration them, I just buoy them in a shallow dish of water with the goal that they may emanate their dazzling scent and permit me to look at them for a couple of days. In a tincture, the entire flowers, leaves, and rings turn a spooky white, and that container has alarmed more than one guest!
There are in excess of 200 types of passionflower on the planet. Fluctuating shades of purple, reds, creams, and white trim the vines. The inside crown can be comprised of straight or wavy spikes that can fluctuate in shading also. The wild **Passiflora**

incarnata is the Tennessee state bloom, and is generally utilized for nourishment and medication. At times called **maypop** (maybe as a result of the manner in which the stems jump out of the ground in May), it delivers a natural product that in my zone (7) still can't seem to ever age adequately to eat.

The unripe foods grown from the ground external skin of the natural product (in any event, when ready) contain cyanide antecedents, of which the smell can now and then be available, and ought not be eaten. Within the organic product, bearing numerous seeds is said to be delectable, yet I can't by and by validate that. Not yet, at any rate.

Despite the fact that the name **passionflower** has a hot undertone, and has once in a while been thought of as a sexual enhancer, the name originates from imagery got from the Christian religion. Its unique name, given by the Cherokees, is ocoee, prompting the Ocoee River and Ocoee River Valley in Tennessee to be named after the plant. Spanish travelers in South America "found" energy flower and named it, seeing strict images in the leaves (hands of Christ's persecutors), (crown of thistles), and five stamens (wounds). Travelers in Peru saw these signs and accepting them as a gift on their endeavor.

Passionflower has woody stems that develop at an astounding rate. Mine bites the dust back to the ground each year, yet the stems arrive at 20 to 30 feet (6 to 9 m) before the finish of summer. The leaves are interchange and palmate (taking after hands), quite often with three projections. The leaves are unmistakable and effectively conspicuous once you've seen them. Gigantic quantities of excellent wavy ringlets help the vine develop and climb. It very well may be very intrusive. It inclines toward incomplete shade, yet full sun doesn't appear to keep it down. Every year there are twice the same numbers of stems jumping from the beginning, along the split-rail fence, and moving up the tall Jerusalem artichoke follows that become close by. In the event that you decide to plant some passionflower vines, do notice this admonition. It requires a great deal of room and moving or expelling it will require watchfulness.

One of the most significant characteristics of passionflower is its capacity to quiet a bustling brain. Individuals who experience difficulty dozing in light of the fact that they go around and around with round deduction, harping on issues, stressing, and worrying, will discover comfort in passionflower.

Promising examination has been done that demonstrates that passionflower can be as compelling on tension as the pharmaceutical diazepam without the unsafe addictive symptoms. Truth be told, passionflower might be extremely useful in decreasing manifestations and trouble with withdrawal and dependence on liquor, nicotine, and different medications. The vast majority of the examination centers around utilizing liquor concentrate of the plant, which is contraindicated for use with liquor dependence, however all things considered the imbuement or tea is made with water.

Utilizing passionflower related to narcotic meds isn't suggested in light of the fact that it might build the activity to an extreme. It is an uterine energizer, so ought to be abstained from during pregnancy.

Passionflower is useful for muscle fits. It may not be the principal thing you'd consider when your back takes care of, yet maybe it ought to be.

This herb likewise quiets the focal sensory system. Levels of synapses, particularly GABA (gamma-aminobutyric corrosive), are expanded, easing back the movement of nerve cells and permitting mental incitement to diminish and unwinding to occur. On account of this action on quieting the nerves, passionflower can be very useful in instances of shingles, particularly related to herbs, for example, St. John's wort and lemon demulcent, when utilized both inside and remotely. It has been utilized for strain and weariness, and a few cultivators feel that it very well may be of help with bringing down circulatory strain. Similarly as with numerous herbs, it can thin the blood to some degree. There have been reports of its utilization for hyperactivity in youngsters with changing degrees of accomplishment.

This mellow yet successful calming and relaxant herb may likewise be of help for asthma and hacks. Local Americans utilized the macerated leaves as a poultice on wounds and wounds and utilized the vines as a tea. Right now, all ethereal parts are utilized restoratively.

Restorative Benefits
- Helps rest
- Quiets nervousness
- Reduces withdrawal indications
- Eases back fits
- Lowers blood pressure
- Alleviates cough and asthma

Calm Candy

The herbs in these sweets help ease uneasiness, stress, and overexcitement.

Ingredients

- 11/2 cups (355 ml) water
- 1/4 cup new passionflower
- 1/4 cup new lemon ointment
- 1/4 cup new chamomile
- Juice and zest of 2 lemons
- Unsalted spread
- 3 cups (600 g) sugar
- 1/2 cup (160 g) corn syrup or honey (if utilizing honey, the sweets will most likely stay clingy) Confectioners' sugar or cornstarch, for sprinkling

Yield: 1 pound (454 g)

Instructions

Join the water, herbs, and lemon squeeze and pizzazz in an enormous pot over medium-low warmth.

Stew to lessen the fluid to 1 cup (235 ml). In the interim, margarine a baking dish.

Include the sugar and corn syrup and mix until the sugar disintegrates. Clasp a treats thermometer to the side of the skillet. Increment the warmth, heat to the point of boiling, and bubble to 300°F (150°C), with as meager blending as could reasonably be expected. Expel from the warmth and empty the hot blend into the baking dish. Let cool.

When it very well may be taken care of, cut into pieces and sprinkle with confectioners' sugar or cornstarch to shield the pieces from staying together. On the other hand, pour onto a spread preparing sheet to 1/4-inch (6 mm) thick, and break into pieces when cooled.

Sleep Time Tea

This evening tea is a decent decision for quite a long time when everybody is excessively drained or experiencing difficulty slowing down. You can utilize the tea instead of water when making gelatin for a sleep time dessert.

Ingredients
- 1 cup (235 ml) water
- 1 teaspoon passionflower
- 1 teaspoon chamomile
- 1 teaspoon lemon salve

Yield: 1 cup (235 ml)

Instructions
Consolidate the water and herbs in a pot and bring to a stew. Expel from the warmth and let steep.

Shower For Restful Sleep

A decent steaming shower implanted with these ingredients alleviates the considerations of the day and their physical appearances.

Ingredients

- 1/4 cup dried passionflower
- 1/4 cup oat straw
- 1/4 cup (90 g) Epsom salts
- Boiling water

Yield: 1 application

Instructions

Spot the ingredients into a muslin pack or tie into the focal point of a washcloth. Ensure the herbs have enough space to mix without any problem. Spot in a 2-quart (2 L) pitcher (unbending plastic is fine). Pour boiling water over the herbs and steep for 10 to 15 minutes while running a shower.

Pour the soaks shower tea and bundle into the tub. Absorb a full tub. The magnesium in the Epsom salts makes an extraordinary expansion to the antispasmodic, loosening up activity of the herbs.

Nighty-Night Elixir

Most botanists will disclose to you that it's ideal to make tinctures as single fixings, and mix them later. That way, in the event that you need one of them with no of different herbs, you have it. When you've mixed them, you're left with the mix.

Ingredients

- 1/2 cup passionflower
- 1/4 cup chamomile
- 1/4 cup lemon analgesic
- 1/4 cup valerian root
- 2 tablespoons skullcap
- 2 tablespoons motherwort
- 1 tablespoon lavender buds
- 4 ounces (112 g) honey
- 1 to 11/2 cups (235 to 355 ml) vodka

Yield: About 11/2 cups (355 ml)

Instructions

Spot all the botanicals in a 16 ounces (470 ml) container. Pour the honey over them and mix to cover them. Include vodka until the container is filled and the plants are submerged.

This blends needs to age for a month. At the point when it's done, strain out the herbs and use around 1 tablespoon (15 ml) of the mixture around 30 minutes before bed.

Passionflower Tea

Passionflower makes an extraordinary tea for loosening up psyche and body without causing you to feel lazy, so it is an incredible tea to drink during the day to enable you to center.

Ingredients

- 2 teaspoons passionflower leaf, vine, and bloom
- 1 cup (235 ml) boiling water
- Honey (discretionary)

Yield: 1 cup (235 ml)

Instructions

Add the herb to the water and steep for 15 minutes. Improve with honey, whenever wanted.

Sleepytime Tea

Blended in with different herbs, passionflower is awesome for a sleepytime tea. This is one of my top picks for having in the night prior to sleep time. This mix quiets the brain, loosens up the nerves, and respites you to rest, empowering a night of soothing rest.

Ingredients

- 1 cup dried passionflower leaf, vine, and flower
- 1/2 cup smooth oats
- 1/4 cup lemon salve leaves
- 1/4 cup chamomile flowers
- 2 tablespoons California poppy aeronautical parts
- 2 tablespoons motherwort leaves
- 1 tablespoon catnip leaves

Yield: 21/4 cups

Instructions

Consolidate the ingredients together and store in a glass container. To utilize, add 1 tablespoon to 1 cup (235 ml) of boiling water. Permit to soak for 15 to 20 minutes. This is best delighted in during or after a hot shower.

Ginger

Zingiber officinale
Zingiberaceae family

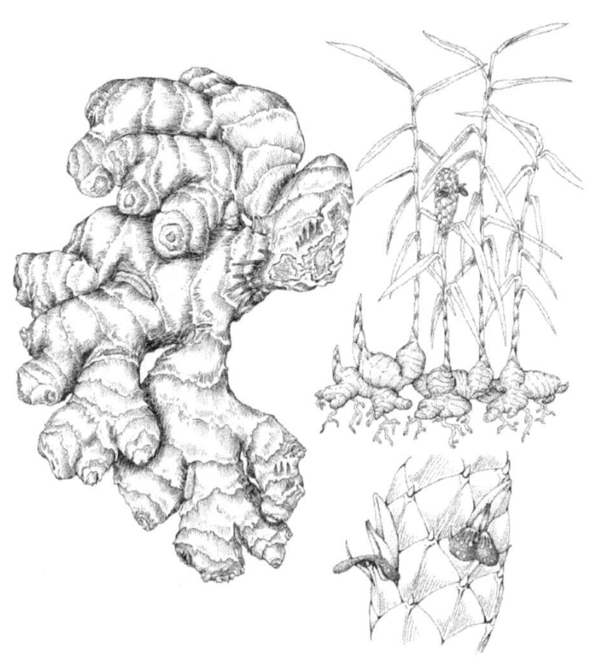

Now, there are in any event five distinct inventions of ginger in my kitchen, and that doesn't check the solidified ginger that is consistently close by, or the granulated zesty hot Chinese honey ginger moment blend that is one of our go-to warm-ups on nippy winter evenings.

Ginger is local to Southeast Asia, and it has been famous for centuries in numerous regions of the world. Ginger is referenced in antiquated Chinese, Indian, and Middle Eastern composition, and is respected for its sweet-smelling, culinary, and therapeutic properties. Antiquated Romans imported ginger from China almost 2,000 years prior. During the 1500s, ginger's utilization spread, disregarding the extraordinary cost of bringing in it from Asia.

Spanish voyagers took ginger toward the West Indies, Mexico, and South America, and in the sixteenth century send out back to Europe initiated to fulfill the extraordinary interest. Jamaica, India, Fiji, Indonesia, and Australia become a large portion of what we use today. Despite the fact that pretty much every other plant in this book is by and large idea of as a weed and can probably be discovered wild in most calm locales, ginger is incorporated in light of the fact that it can undoubtedly be developed right in the kitchen.

It takes a year or two to grow a consistent source, however it's justified, despite all the trouble. Here's the secret:

1. First you need some great soil. Ginger will develop in rich soil that holds dampness, however there must likewise be acceptable seepage. You won't need the dirt to dry out between waterings, yet it ought to be sodden, not wet.
2. Pick new stout "hands" from the merchant, and drench for the time being. They can be cut into pieces or planted entirety. A 12-inch (30.5 cm) measurement pot will deal with around three great size hands.
3. Plant them 3 inches (7.5 cm) profound with the buds looking up.
4. Spot the pot where there is acceptable daylight, however not in direct light; it doesn't need to hoard all your great windowsill space.
5. When set up, you can simply uncover what you need when you need it. It's ideal to disregard it for a year to get it entrenched, however.

To freeze extra ginger, grind the ginger altogether. Include a teaspoon or two of water or lemon juice, just to expand dampness. Press solidly into ice 3D square plate, and freeze. At the point when solidified, pop them out and place into a cooler sack, crushing out the overabundance air. Presently you have ginger prepared when you need it.

There are numerous gingers in the Zingiberaceae family. The three most normal are Zingiber officinale, which is the customary ginger; Curcuma longa, known as turmeric; and Alpinia galanga, called galangal. Of these three, ginger and turmeric have been found as of late to have practically boundless advantages for human wellbeing, offering solutions for everything from a resentful stomach to potentially restoring or forestalling malignancy. I expect that very soon we'll be taking in progressively about advantages from galangal. These roots are fabulous, staggeringly wellbeing giving, and flavorfully simple to add to the eating regimen each and every day. Other huge exceptional gingers are cardamom (**Elettaria cardamomum**) and zedoary (**Curcurma zedoaria**).

Since finding ginger's capacity to clear queasiness immediately, I once in a while experience the ill effects of it as long as I have ginger nearby. I offered a cousin taking a journey a baggie of ginger root containers with directions to utilize them in the event that she got nauseous. Every so often into the outing, the boat hit difficult situations. She later disclosed to me that she was one of not many making the rounds on the decks.
When added to different herbs—in teas, tinctures, or syrups, for example—ginger initiates them.
Ginger is an energizer, and it advances course, assisting with getting things going. It is a profoundly compelling mitigating, and on the grounds that irritation is behind so much deadly infections, particularly in our veins and significant organs, ginger can be exceptionally helpful. Anti-microbial and antibacterial, it battles bacterial sicknesses and may be helpful (preemptively) against impacts of gamma radiation. It is additionally antifungal.

Ginger offers relief from discomfort similarly cayenne does, and can be utilized remotely in analgesics, balms, and liniments on sore joints and muscles. Utilized inside for pain, ginger concentrate has been demonstrated to be as powerful as ibuprofen for menstrual agony and in the same class as or better than a portion of the pharmaceutical medications utilized for gout, osteoarthritis in the knees, and rheumatoid joint inflammation, without the lethal reactions. It underpins heart wellbeing too. Furthermore, it is flavorful! Hardly any heated desserts go into our broiler without some finely minced solidified ginger mixed into the player first. It lights up nearly everything.

There are some medication associations to know about when utilizing ginger routinely or in huge amount, so examine it with your doctor on the off chance that you are utilizing heart prescriptions, NSAIDS, drug for diabetes, or a blood-diminishing medicine.

Restorative Benefits
- Treats queasiness
- Promotes dissemination
- Reduces irritation
- Kills microorganisms, parasites, and different pathogens
- Relieves pain (inward and outer)

Spicy Ginger Elixir

I began making this when there was extra ginger. To start with, it was only a ginger tincture; however it steadily turned into this tasty mix that can be taken alone by the dropperful, or added to boiling water or herbal tea to jazz it up with refreshing properties. It has never had a careful formula; however this is a decent beginning stage.

Ingredients

- 1/2 cup (50 g) hacked ginger
- 1 lemon, daintily cut
- 1 (4-inch, or 10 cm) cinnamon stick
- 2 star anise
- 2 cardamom units
- 1/2 cup (160 g) crude nearby honey
- 1 cup (235 ml) 100 proof vodka or liquor

Yield: 1 cup (235 ml)

Instructions

Spot the ginger, lemon cuts, cinnamon, star anise, cardamom and honey into a 16 ounces container, mix to join, and add the vodka to cover (it might take more or under 1 cup [235 ml]). Permit to soak for about a month. Strain into a spotless container and appreciate.

Solid Morning Muffins

These wheat biscuits contain no sugar, however with the fruit purée and banana you won't notice. There's bunches of supporting goodness here to begin the day on an even note. They freeze well, as well.

Ingredients

- 1 cup (120 g) wheat grain
- 1 cup (120 g) oat wheat
- 1 cup (120 g) whole wheat flour
- 2 teaspoons baking powder
- 1 teaspoon baking pop
- 2 tablespoons (12 g) minced new ginger
- 1/2 teaspoon cinnamon
- 1/2 teaspoon nutmeg
- 1 cup (245 g) fruit purée
- 1 squashed ready banana
- 1/2 cup (120 ml) skim milk
- 2 egg whites, gently beaten
- 2 tablespoons (30 ml) olive oil

Yield: 12 biscuits

Instructions

Preheat the broiler to 400°F (200°C, or gas mark 6). Line a 12-cup biscuit tin with paper liners.

In an enormous bowl, join the wheat and oat grains, entire wheat flour, baking powder, preparing pop, ginger, cinnamon, and nutmeg. In another bowl, consolidate the fruit purée, banana, milk, egg whites, and oil. Empty the wet ingredients into the dry ingredients and blend until simply consolidated. Partition uniformly among the readied biscuit cups.

Prepare for 14 to 16 minutes, or until a toothpick embedded into the middle comes out clingy however not wet.

Cool on a wire rack.

Banana Ginger Bread

The ginger adds shimmer to the flavors in this cakelike bread, making it a most loved at our home.

Ingredients

- 2 cups (240 g) universally handy flour
- 3/4 teaspoon baking soda
- 1/2 teaspoon salt
- 1/2 cup (100 g) sugar
- 1/4 cup (56 g) unsalted margarine, relaxed
- 2 enormous eggs
- 11/2 cups (338 g) pounded ready banana (around 3 bananas)
- 1/4 cup (80 g) plain yogurt
- 2 tablespoons minced solidified ginger
- 1 teaspoon vanilla concentrate

Yield: 1loaf

Instructions

Preheat the broiler to 350°F (180°C, or gas mark 4). Oil a 81/2 × 41/2-inch (21.5 × 11.5 cm) portion skillet.

Join the flour, baking pop, and salt in a bowl and mix with a whisk. With a blender, cream the sugar and margarine together in an enormous bowl. Include the eggs, 1 at once, beating admirably after every expansion.

Include the banana, yogurt, ginger, and vanilla. Mix well.

Include the flour blend gradually and beat at low speed just until damp. Spoon the player into the readied dish. Heat for 60 minutes, or until a wooden toothpick embedded into the middle tells the truth.

Cool in the dish on a wire rack for 10 minutes. Expel from the container and cool totally on the wire rack.

Note:
In the event that utilizing new minced ginger root, increase the sugar by 1/4 cup (50 g).

Ginger Mint Liniment

My preferred use for this liniment is on tired feet and calves in the wake of a monotonous day of standing.

Ingredients

- 1/4 cup (25 g) ground new ginger
- 11/4 cups (295 ml) olive oil
- 5 to 10 drops peppermint fundamental oil

Yield: 1 cup (235 ml)

Instructions

Warmth the ginger and the olive oil together over the least warmth setting for as long as 60 minutes. Expel from the warmth and permit to rest for the time being. Strain the cooled oil through an espresso channel to evacuate all solids.

Include the fundamental oil. Fill bottles. Back rub into sore regions tenderly to diminish pain.

Ginger Bath

This invigorating drench will help with drained, sore muscles.

Ingredients
1 cup (100 g) ground or cut ginger

Yield: 1 application

Instructions
Spot the ginger in a muslin sack and tie safely. Spot the muslin sack in a tub of high temp water and steep for 10 minutes. Or on the other hand, join the sack to the spigot and permit high temp water to go through it. Absorb the hot shower for 20 to 30 minutes.

Plantain

Plantago major and Plantago lanceolata
Plantaginaceae family

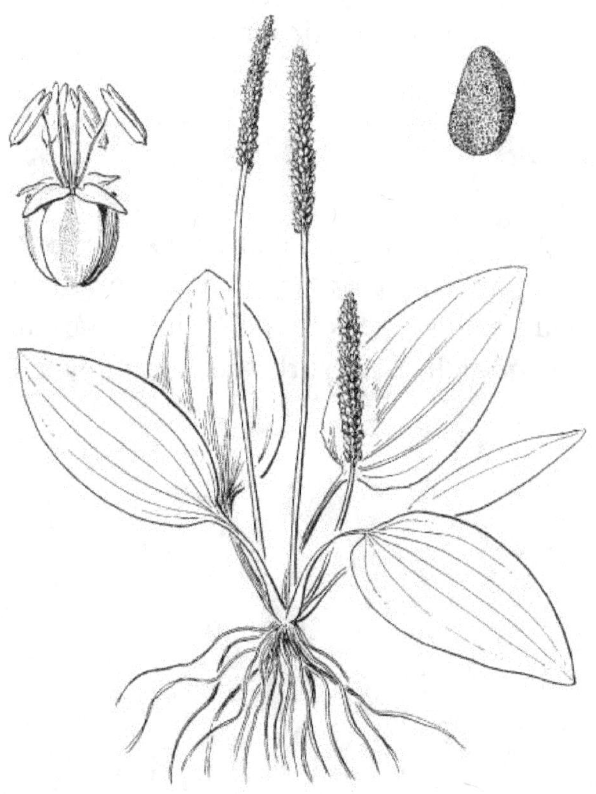

Taking PLANTAIN up in conversation with a room brimming with herb fans and you'll be astounded at how much energy you'll discover for a humble yard weed that a large number of individuals spend a fortune attempting to annihilate. The two basic assortments are P. major and P. lanceolata, and they have numerous monikers: ribwort, narrowleaf plantain, English plantain, buckhorn plantain, lanceleaf plantain, ribgrass, and some more. In my youth they were "bunny's ears" and I've heard individuals call them "pig ears" and "garden lettuce," among others.

Plantain develops all around the world. It is imagined that it was naturalized to a limited extent through pollution of grain bound for seeding during harvest and planted right alongside the grain in new fields in new places.

There are in excess of 200 types of plantain, yet I will concentrate on these two, the most popular, least demanding to discover, and generally utilized. They are exchangeable to such an extent that other than a depiction, I won't separate between P. major and P. lanceolata. They are enduring weeds developing from a little rosette that turns out to be very rich. In semishaded secured places, I've seen the leaves of both become in excess of 6 inches (15.2 cm) long, and P. major almost as wide. P. lanceolata can get over a foot (30.5 cm) long.

Normally about the day after you cut your garden, their seed stalks (inflorescences) spring up 4 or 5 inches (10 or 12.5 cm), and P. major has long spikes of seeds while P. lanceolata bears shorter, cone-molded seed heads on the dainty, whiplike stems. In one more day or two, sensitive rings of minor, rich white flowers open on the spikes. Now, your garden looks quite worn out. In any event mine does. Between the plantain and the dandelions, I swear I can hear the neighbors moan when they walk around.

This is another plant that can make you fully aware of the supernatural occurrence like forces of herbs. Antibacterial, astringent, calming, sterile, demulcent, diuretic, expectorant, purgative, and refrigerant are only the start of the rundown of advantages from this plant. The leaves, seeds, and roots are completely esteemed in medication, and the leaves (especially youthful, delicate leaves) are a great expansion to servings of mixed greens or cooked as a vegetable like spinach; they contain heaps of basic minerals, calcium, iron, potassium, and vitamins A, C, K, B1, riboflavin, and carotenes with a generally low measure of oxalic corrosive. Those dull green leaves are loaded with acceptable wellbeing.

Plantain offers quick alleviation for honey bee stings. Cleave it or squash it and warmth it quickly on the off chance that you can. It will dissuade expanding and pain. Plantain contains aucubin, a neutralizing agent; notwithstanding pulling out the venom, it really attempts to stop the venom's belongings.

Plantain additionally contains allantoin, which advances wound mending, speeds cell recovery, and has emollient and calming impacts. Plantain is sheltered to eat or take inside, and that is extremely welcome news. It has styptic properties also. Wounds to the whole stomach related framework can profit by ingesting one of the numerous types of plantain—as a tea, tincture, soup or stock, or vegetable.

The seed husks of plantain will, when wet, grow and ooze adhesive, encouraging simpler end of the entrails by expanding in the gut and going about as a mass diuretic while calming bothering en route. Economically, seeds of P. psyllium are reaped explicitly for this reason, and the powdered seeds and husks are the principle fixing in Metamucil. P. psyllium has the most elevated level of adhesive, however the plantain seeds developing in your yard are very sufficient. P. psyllium will draw out dampness, which is useful in moving the entrails.

The leaves are emollient, and are frequently utilized in teas, syrups, or tinctures for sinus blockage, hacks, a wide range of stomach objections, center ear contaminations, and the sky is the limit from there. The root is said to have been utilized for toothache and snakebite. Those two things sound altogether different except if you think about that in the two cases, poisons should be pulled out. Poultices are utilized for everything from splinters, burns from the sun, rashes, cuts, and scratches to reports of bygone era use on tumors.

In late ages, the utilization of plantain has gotten for the most part outside. Ointments, cleansers, emollients, and arrangements of various sorts are promptly accessible, thus we've quit considering it nourishment or an inner medication. I feel that is exceptionally dismal, considering all it brings to the table us.

Have plantain good to go. Here are some basic approaches to keep it close by:

Dry plantain leaves in summer to keep close by. Lay on a screen in a cool, dim spot. At the point when totally dry, store in a fixed container.

Infuse olive oil with plantain leaves, new or dry. There are countless approaches to utilize this oil: legitimately on the skin, blended in with vinegar for serving of mixed greens dressing, in medicine, in the shower, or after a shower. You will think about how you lived without it, particularly on the off chance that you live in a region with dry air.

Make a solid mixture of plantain in water, and afterward freeze into ice blocks. Void 3D shapes into a capacity compartment and keep solidified until prepared to utilize.

Steep some plantain vinegar. Utilize great quality vinegar so it tends to be utilized both inside and remotely. Not refined white, alright? Fill a container freely with new, clean plantain leaves. On the off chance that you'd prefer to incorporate a few roots, that is fine as well, yet for the most part leaves. Spread with vinegar and spot a nonreactive top on the compartment. Permit to soak inconclusively, stressing it when you're prepared to utilize it. You may utilize the vinegar in a serving of mixed greens dressing, to splash on burn from the sun, or to use as a hair or facial flush to relieve and keep up a solid pH balance. A spoonful of vinegar blended in with water or squeeze every day could be useful with incessant bronchitis, sore throats, tireless hacks, and horde stomach related problems.

Restorative Benefits

- Kills microscopic organisms and different pathogens

- Tightens tissues
- Reduces aggravation
- Soothes mucous layers
- Stimulates pee
- Loosens bodily fluid
- Facilitates defecations
- Reduces internal heat level
- Heals and calms wounds and stings

Fried Plantain Greens

Accumulate youth leaves, close to 4 inches (10 cm) long.

Ingredients

- 3 tablespoons (45 ml) toasted sesame oil
- 1 scallion, minced
- 1 quart plantain leaves

Yield: 4 servings

Instructions

Warmth the oil in a skillet over medium warmth and include the scallion. After the scallion begins to relax, include the plantain leaves and cook, blending regularly, just until they wither marginally and are warmed through.

Plantain Field Poultice

I frequently hear the expression "spit poultice," and that is truly what this is. On account of a honey bee sting, mosquito or creepy crawly nibble, annoy sting, or toxic substance oak/ivy/sumac presentation, put a couple of leaves of plantain in your mouth and bite sufficiently long to separate the leaf structure and saturate with the goal that it can shape to the injury or region.

Rolling the leaves firmly in your grasp or between your fingers will have a similar impact, in spite of the fact that the spit truly helps hold it together.

PLANTAIN SKIN CARE

I love the skin-recovering properties of plantain and use it widely in my healthy skin line. It very well may be utilized as either an oil imbuement or a water extricate (decoction).

The since a long time ago leafed assortment specifically is anything but difficult to assemble.

The simplest strategy for a do-it-yourselfer is to make a salve for dried out lips or skin. To do this, mix your dried plantain in oil, for example, olive oil, sunflower oil, or almond oil. Blend your injected oil in with cocoa spread and beeswax. The sums ought to be around 60 percent injected oil, 20 percent cocoa butter and 20 percent beeswax. Or then again for a rearranged formula, attempt the accompanying.

Ingredients
- 3 tablespoons (45 ml) plantain-mixed oil
- 1 tablespoon (14 g) cocoa butter
- 1 tablespoon (14 g) beeswax

Yield: 5 tablespoons (75 g)

Instructions

In a pot, heat all the ingredients delicately over low warmth until liquefied. Mix together and fill tins. Let cement before putting tops on the tins. In the event that you need a demulcent that is fewer firms, utilize less beeswax.

Plantain Tea

Plantain tea has a conventional taste alone, yet it is amazing blended in with lemon demulcent. The adhesive properties of plantain additionally help facilitate an irritated stomach.

Ingredients
- 1 teaspoon dried plantain leaf
- 1 teaspoon dried lemon salve leaf
- 1 cup boiling water (235 ml)

Yield: 1 serving

Instructions
Consolidate the herbs in a tea infuser. Pour boiling water over and let steep for 5 minutes. Drink.

Rose

Rosa spp.
Rosaceae family

THE LORE concerning roses is broad. The term **subrosa** occurred in Roman occasions when a rose was hung topsy turvy over the supper table, implying that the discussions held were to be kept classified. A rose painted on a sign turned into the image for the medieval art of pharmacist. William Shakespeare frequently remembered references to roses for his composition. It is said that Cleopatra secured the floors of her royal residence knee-profound with flower petals to allure Mark Antony, and the sails of her burst were absorbed rose water. The ruler Nero was so enchanted of roses that he had an establishment that spritzed rose water onto supper visitors during feasts, and the roof opened to drop flower petals onto the visitors. Wild roses are a piece of numerous Native American plans, and rose hips were a significant nourishment hotspot for some clans.
In the Ojibwe language, the word for rose hips is **oginiiminagaawanzh,** which means "mother organic product from a little bramble."

At different focuses ever, roses have been worn as crowns, dispersed before eminence and ladies, eaten, intoxicated, and even utilized in the mortar of structures. Uncommon is an affection elixir or spell that does exclude rose. Pliny the Elder recorded in excess of thirty therapeutic uses for rose during the principal century AD. Roses have been developed and utilized for a considerable length of time.

The Rosaceae family is huge and is all the time lined up with the heart, both truly and inwardly. There are in excess of 10,000 rose species, fluctuating from the little white multi-vegetation rose those fragrances the byways and valleys close to my home in late-winter to the exquisite cabbage roses, for example, Centifolia, Damask, Gallica, Cannina, and tea roses, and thousands in the middle. Roses come in numerous structures, sizes, hues, and even aromas.

The unpredictable oil in rose (just as in excess of 100 distinguished constituents—up until now) has many recuperating properties; it is upper, profoundly cell reinforcement, antispasmodic, Spanish fly, astringent, antibacterial, antiviral, sterile, firmly mitigating, blood tonic, purging, cooling, stomach related energizer, expectorant, bile creation energizer, kidney tonic, and menstrual controller, making this fragrant excellence an all out medication bureau on a stem.

Its astringent properties make rose a decent expansion to a tea or rinse for an irritated throat.

Antibacterial and antiviral, it can help battle diseases of the intestinal tract. It is likewise an extraordinary help for the safe framework, making it significant in instances of cold or influenza. Rose water has been utilized for a long time for the skin, and the tea or a poultice of the leaves and petals can be an alleviating and renewing facial. Flower petal vinegar assuages the agony of burn from the sun and makes an awesome hair wash just as a captivating element for dressings or sauces, so make certain to imbue a few petals in vinegar. Flower petal tea or treatment produced using imbuing petals in oil is incredible for rashes and dry, sore skin.

More than everything else, rose encourages open the heart to trust. It eases uneasiness and is a cooling, quieting tonic for the nerves. For individuals battling with self-uncertainty, nervousness, or perimenopause, rose will mitigate the pressure and bolster the organs that need to discharge the poisons these feelings toss into the circulation system.

I have a whole slope planted with **Rosa rugosa**. The primary year or two there were goats living on a similar slope, and the flowers were kept excessively all around manicured. Presently without goat, the dark green leaves burst forward in May followed by surges of red, pink, and white blooms with a fragrance that almost feigns exacerbation back in my mind. I accumulate whatever number as would be prudent, feeling that the more prominent the scent, the more grounded the medication.

In the fall, I accumulate the full rose hips for use in cleanser and syrups. The flavor is somewhat better after an ice, however I attempt to get them while they are still full so I can strip the external, usable part away effectively from the thick inside bundle of bushy seeds. The pieces of the profound orange tissue, ideal for teas or syrup, are then dried and put away in a firmly shut holder in a cool dull spot. The tart hips are an extraordinary wellspring of vitamin C just as A, B, D, and E. Rose hips are additionally pressed with bioflavonoids and have about the entirety of the therapeutic properties of the petals. Rose hip seed oil is a fixed oil (not fundamental) that is famous for mending or forestalling scar tissue; it recovers skin, forestalls wrinkles, calms psoriasis and dermatitis, recuperates consumes, and enables harmed skin to recapture its characteristic tone and shading.

Restorative Benefits
- Lifts discouragement
- Inhibits oxidation
- Relieves muscle fits
- Boosts moxie
- Constricts tissue
- Kills microscopic organisms, infections, and different pathogens
- Reduces aggravation
- Stimulates processing
- Loosens mucus
- Increases bile creation

Rose And Lemon Gulkand

Rose gulkand is a sort of rose jam that began in the Middle East, where it is utilized to animate assimilation. It is cooling and diminishes pressure. It is additionally heavenly. I began including lemon, and discover it about compelling.

Ingredients

- 1 quart (1 L) softly pressed profoundly fragrant flower petals 11/2 to 2 cups (300 to 400 g) crude sugar
- Zest of 1 lemon
- 1/8 teaspoon ground cardamom

Yield: 1 quart (1 L)

Instructions

In a perfect quart (1 L) container, layer 1 inch (2.5 cm) of flower petals. Spread with around 1/4 inch (6 mm) of sugar. Rehash. Each couple of layers, include a touch of the lemon zest and a spot of the cardamom. Proceed until all the ingredients are utilized, with sugar being the top layer. Spread firmly.

Leave on the windowsill, where the daylight will separate the petals and the sugar and rose will start to merge. Each and every other day, mix the blend and return it to the windowsill. Proceed for a month, and it is finished.

This is flavorful on scones, frozen yogurt, crepes, and even toast. The fragile kind of rose with the dash of the lemon and smoothness of the cardamom is life-changing. This could undoubtedly be viewed as an affection spell if that goal is included during the mixing. Feed it to the object of your expressions of love—it could very well work.

Rose Milk Bath

The accompanying formula can be made with any sort of powdered milk. Goat, dairy animals, and coconut milk are for the most part accessible in powdered structure. Another choice is to include 1 cup (235 ml) of new milk legitimately to the shower and blend the rose blend independently, which would permit the utilization of soy or nut drains too, in the event that you like. Utilizing powdered milk lets you imagine everything ahead and it can even be bundled for blessings, yet whichever way works fine.

Ingredients
2 cups flower petals (the most fragrant you can discover)
2 cups violet leaves
2 cups (240 g) milk powder
1/2 cup (40 g) cereal

Yield: 12 to 14 applications

Instructions
Join all the ingredients in a water/air proof container. To utilize, place around 1/4 cup of the blend into a material sack and mix it in simply bubbled water for 10 minutes while the shower runs. Pour the tea (and the pack) into the tub and drench your considerations away. Soothing to dry or desolate skin.

Rose Beads

There are a few old plans for rose dots that include cooking the petals for a few days in cast iron. This strategy produces coal dark globules. They are beautiful, and I've made them a couple of times, yet I am not the patient kind. To make rose dabs in a single day (with the exception of the drying), follow this formula.

Ingredients

- 1 tablespoon finely powdered flower petals (the most profound shading you can discover is ideal)
- 1/4 teaspoon gum tragacanth powder
- 1/2 teaspoon red or pink earth
- 1 tablespoon (15 ml) rose water, or more varying

Instructions

In a bowl, mix the powders and include the rose water. The consistency ought to take after demonstrating earth. Fold the dots with your fingers into the size and shape that you'd like, and string them onto thick wire. I utilize botanical wire from the specialty store, the thickest accessible. Leave around 1/2 inch (1.3 cm) between globules.

Wrap the wires of dots over a case or bowl so that there is course underneath the dabs. Tenderly pivot the dabs on the wire each 8 or 10 hours. Contingent upon the size of the dabs you make, they may be dry the following day, or it could take a few days.

Rose And Vanilla Elixir

Favored Maine Herb Farm was granted in front of the rest of the competition for this remedy in the Simply Delicious Syrups and Elixirs class at the 2013 International Herb Symposium.
Roses elevate the soul, quiet and focus the psyche, feed the heart, and support love and reproduction. They are astringent and tonic to the stomach related and eliminative tract. Vanilla beans unwind and calm, warm the gut, bring us into our bodies, offer gentle love potion properties, and taste delectable.

Ingredients

- 3 to 5 vanilla beans, cut the long way and finely hacked or squeezed 1-16 ounces (470 ml) container approximately loaded up with new flower petals 1 cup (235 ml) excellent, smooth-tasting liquor.
- 1 cup (320 g) unadulterated crude honey

Instructions

Add the vanilla to the container of roses. Consolidate the liquor and honey, blend well, and pour over the roses and vanilla. Spread to the edge of the container and jab with a chopstick to ensure the herbal material is secured. Top the container and store in a cool, dim spot for 4 to about a month and a half. Strain and tap into a perfect jug.
Take a dropperful of the mixture straight into your mouth, or add to some hot or cold water or tea whenever you need a touch of motivation, unwinding, or break. It's a phenomenal gut-warming stomach related guide and is great over vanilla frozen yogurt!

Raspberry Blackberry

Rubus spp.
Rosaceae family

There are many wild berries that spread the slopes, fencerows, and forests, yet the most commonplace and handily recognized are raspberries and blackberries. Other than being delectable, they have numerous restorative properties.

Raspberry time is around midsummer. Blackberries mature close to the finish of the midyear.

With a little ingenuity, you can discover wild products of the soil nourishments nearly all year, contingent upon the atmosphere. The raspberries that develop wild in my general vicinity are "dark raspberries" since they are dark when ready (Rubus occidentalis). Red raspberry leaf (Rubus idaeus) is utilized restoratively, yet the dark ones have a significant part of similar properties and a lot of the important cell reinforcements that make such huge numbers of the red, blue, and purple berries "superfoods." The shades in these nourishments are anthocyanins, a normally happening flavonoid, and they have a lot to offer.

Numerous in the clinical field accept that about all infection is brought about by irritation and the means our body's resistance instruments take to battle it. Anthocyanins are credited with battling the free radicals that lead to aggravation. The berries are additionally antiviral and anticancer, help keep up a sound pulse and forestall coronary illness, and may even secure against stoutness.

Raspberries and blackberries are total natural products made out of some little, single-seeded drupelets. The drupelets structure around the outside of a center, or grate. At the point when raspberries are picked, the berry sneaks off the scratch, deserting it, and there is a space in the natural product where the grate was.

Raspberries are adjusted. With blackberries (Rubus fruticosus), the repository severs and stays inside the natural product. At the point when a ready blackberry is picked, the stem abandoned is spotless and level, and the delicate white center remains inside the berry. The blackberry isn't empty. In the event that it isn't ready, it won't leave away effectively from the stem. Blackberries are elliptical or even to some degree barrel shaped. It came as an incredible astonishment to find that the leaves of these natural products (just as those of strawberry) make a tea that is carefully enhanced like the organic product. Raspberry leaf tea has numerous awesome restorative employments.

A standout amongst other known is for conditioning the uterus and facilitating labor, because of its capacity to loosen up veins and help unwind (or contract) smooth muscle. Maternity specialists frequently prescribe it throughout the previous scarcely any long stretches of pregnancy, and it is conceivable that a conditioned, loosened up uterus is increasingly open to undeveloped organism implantation, settling on it a decent prepregnancy decision for those wishing to imagine. Wellbeing of utilization in the ahead of schedule to late phase of pregnancy is blended, so I would by and by decide to maintain a strategic distance from it until half a month preceding the due date.

Raspberry leaf teas, just as the organic products, are cooling in the warmth of summer. I appreciate drying the additional foods grown from the ground them coarsely to add to tea mixes. The berries are stacked with vitamin C and dietary fiber. The leaves have significantly more to offer, including vitamins A and B mind boggling, iron, calcium, magnesium, phosphorous, and potassium. It very well may be useful for leg cramps.

Blackberry has a long history of utilization, especially among Native Americans who utilized root and leaf decoctions for looseness of the bowels. Some pre-owned it for hemorrhoids and lung conditions, also. Old Greeks utilized blackberry for gout, so one of its numerous epithets is the goutberry. Another is brambleberry, due to the wild development propensity for the blackberry. The sticks can develop more than 15 feet (5 m) long in a solitary season, and the thorns some of the time take over immense territories of a few sections of land.
Blackberry leaf and root bark are both viewed as the restorative pieces of the plant. The leaf and root bark are astringent, diuretic, and wealthy in tannins. They have for quite some time been utilized in instances of looseness of the bowels and for oral

(mucous film) irritation. Hemorrhoids react to outside utilization of blackberry as a pack or wash.

My granddad was not a lot of a consumer; however blackberry cognac was a top pick. I make my own rendition by filling a container with new, ready berries, a couple of leaves, and some root bark, and afterward covering it totally with cognac for in any event a little while before stressing it for use.

Make certain to assemble and dry some wild berries and leaves for wild teas loaded with vitamins and flavor over the winter. The leaves are anything but difficult to dry on a screen. Ensure they are totally dry before putting away. The berries can be somewhat harder, however. I normally put them in a solitary layer on a treat sheet fixed with preparing material, and put them in the broiler on "warm" for a few hours until they have begun to dry. They contain a great deal of water, so in the event that they aren't dried cautiously and rapidly, they can form. The warm stove strategy has not bombed me yet.

Restorative Benefits
- Reduces irritation
- Kills infections
- Prevents malignant growth
- Reduces hypertension
- Prevents coronary illness
- Protects against weight
- Eases labor
- Eases cramps
- Treats gout

- Constricts tissues
- Promotes pee

Berry Fruit Leather

We have an excellent Golden Delicious apple tree, so I generally make fruit purée first, and afterward utilize that as a base for natural product cowhide. It comes out uniform and sweet, and the fruit purée holds the juices from berries that probably won't have enough substance to make decent calfskin. You can utilize locally acquired fruit purée similarly too. Unsweetened is bounty sweet once it dries down.

Ingredients

- 1/2 to 1 cup (120 to 235 ml) berry juice (can be one berry or blended)
- 2 cups (490 g) fruit purée

Yield: 12 × 18-inch (30.5 × 45.7 cm) sheet, cut into segments based on your personal preference

Instructions

Preheat the broiler to the most minimal setting.

To make the juice, crush the berries with a good old potato masher or spoon, and warmth in a pot until the juice runs. Squash well. Strain to get all the juice accessible and evacuate the seeds. Mix with the fruit purée.

Line a huge shallow-sided treat sheet with material paper. A few people utilize plastic wrap, which is tidier, yet warmed plastic is anything but an especially solid decision. Spread the mixed juice and fruit purée to a uniform thickness on the treat sheet, close to 1/4-inch (6 mm) thick.

Place in the broiler for a few hours. Check regularly, and if essential, pivot the dish. The focal point of the blend ought to be marginally tasteless, however not wet when it is done.

To store, cut into strips, lay on somewhat bigger pieces of waxed paper, and move up. Keep in a firmly fixed container. Refrigerate, or eat inside half a month.

Black Raspberry Pie

At the point when Mom heated, it was an occasion. Her baking time was seriously limited, having a board of telephones ringing 24 hours every day and five children to raise, yet sporadically, we discovered enough dark raspberries, and she discovered sufficient opportunity to prepare them into a pie.

Ingredients

- Cake for a 8-inch (20 cm) two-covering pie
- 3/4 cup (150 g) sugar
- 1/4 cup (30 g) flour
- 1/4 teaspoon ground cinnamon
- 3 cups (435 g) new dark raspberries
- 1 tablespoon (14 g) unsalted spread

Yield: 8 servings

Instructions

Preheat the stove to 425°F (220°C, or gas mark 7). Line a pie container with one of the outsides.

In a bowl, consolidate the sugar, flour, and cinnamon. Include the berries and blend daintily. Fill the cake lined pie container. Dab with the spread. Spread with the top covering. Seal and woodwind. Prick the outside layer with a fork.

Prepare until the covering is brilliant earthy colored and the juices are bubbly and thickened, 35 to 45 minutes.

ACCEPT THE WAY THINGS ARE FOR MEN

This mix advances sound prostate capacity and standardizes pee stream. It consolidates various strong herbs. This formula may likewise be useful for an amplified prostate.

Ingredients
- 2 cups (290 g) red raspberries
- Unsalted margarine or coconut oil, for lubing
- 1/4 ounce dried ashwagandah
- 1/4 ounce dried saw palmetto
- 1/4 ounce dried powdered turmeric
- 1/4 ounce dried gotu kola
- 1/4 ounce dried annoy
- 1/4 ounce dried raspberry leaf
- 2 cups (400 g) natural sugar or (640 g) honey

Yield: The yield is reliant on the size of your drops. I make some bigger for grown-ups and some littler for youngsters.

Instructions

Make a juice from the berries. In a pot, spread the raspberries with water in addition to 1 inch (2.5 cm), and bubble until the berries have popped. Strain. Put aside 1 cup (235 ml).

Oil a shape with spread or coconut oil. On the off chance that you don't have a shape, you will roll the sweets later.

In a little hardened steel pot, heat up the ashwagandah, saw palmetto, and turmeric in water to cover for 25 minutes. On the off chance that the fluid gets low, include more water in 1/4 cup (60 ml) increases. Mood killer the warmth and include the guto kola, annoy and raspberry leaf. Let sit, secured, for 25 minutes. Cool and strain the blend utilizing cheesecloth. Hold 1/2 cup (120 ml) of the tea and manure the herbs.

In a pot, join the sugar, saved berry fluid, and held tea; heat to the point of boiling. Cook the blend, mixing continually, until the syrup arrives at 290° to 300°F (143° to 150°C) on a sweets thermometer (this will take some time). Spot a drop or two of the syrup into a bowl brimming with ice water. On the off chance that the syrup turns and remains hard (split stage), at that point you know it's prepared. On the off chance that it is still delicate and clingy, it needs to continue cooking.

Empty the syrup into the molds. You can expel the drops from the shape once they have cooled. In the event that you don't have a shape, when the syrup has cooled and is malleable, start pulling off little pieces and moving between the palms of your lubed hands, framing a little ball. Work rapidly in light of the fact that the blend solidifies really quick. Store in a cool, dry spot.

Sage

Salvia spp.
Labiatae family

There are quite a few cultivars and types of salvia. More often than not when we talk about sage, we're depicting garden sage, yet the white stylized sage from the desert Southwest, the striking pineapple sage that draws hummingbirds, the tall, copiously blooming Mexican bramble sage, the tremendous, pompous clary sage, and all the assortments in the middle of likewise have their own employments.

A few sages are predominantly fancy, some are developed for their fragrance, many are stunning medication, and some make breathtaking tea. We don't think about this culinary herb so frequently as we ought to in cooking. It has a great deal to offer. Sage leaves are solid and thick with a surface that shows up pebbled. They help me to some degree to remember a misrepresented tongue. Since it is astringent, it helps recoil excited mucous films of the mouth and throat.

Sage contains a wide scope of significant and mending unstable oils, flavonoids (counting apigenin, diosmetin, and luteolin), and phenolic acids, including rosmarinic corrosive, found in the herb rosemary.

This corrosive is promptly accessible for ingestion in the gastrointestinal tract and from that point can lessen the quantity of incendiary informing atoms, along these lines assisting with decreasing irritation. Also, sage contains cancer prevention agent catalysts that consolidate with the flavonoids and acids, giving it an extraordinary capacity to settle harm to cells from free radicals. Because of this exceptional mix, sage is a ground-breaking herb for individuals with conditions brought about by or intensified by aggravation, for example, rheumatoid joint pain, asthma, and atherosclerosis.

The name Salvia gets from the Latin salvere, signifying "to be spared" or "salvation." There are numerous herbs that lead me not far off of pondering which started things out, the herb or the word. Sage is one such herb. At the point when we utilize the word sage in a non-herbal setting, it alludes to one who holds a lot of astuteness. We search for "wise counsel." So it is intriguing without a doubt that eating sage upgrades memory because of the flavonoids and in all probability rosmarinic corrosive.

Sage is an astonishing wellspring of a few B-complex vitamins, including folic corrosive, thiamin, pyridoxine, and riboflavin. A lot of vitamins C and An, or more minerals like potassium, zinc, calcium, iron, manganese, copper, and magnesium, make this an important nourishment route past what it can accomplish for a turkey a few times each year!

Nursery sage (Salvia officinalis) and the numerous assortments of Salvia are utilized whenever there is a plenitude of dampness. Moms wishing to evaporate milk creation have depended on sage for a considerable length of time.

Menopausal hot flashes now and again react to sage tea or tincture. Colds where there is a great deal of bodily fluid can profit by sage. Sage is additionally quieting and establishing both inside and remotely. It has generally been utilized to treat fevers and advance rest.

Clary sage, Salvia sclarea

The herb is seen as equipped for murdering E. coli and is a solid antifungal. Utilizing powdered sage in items, for example, natively constructed toothpaste, liniments, or vinegars can take care of numerous issues because of clamminess, sweat, and organism. An imbued vinegar is dynamite on sleek skin or as a hair flush for slick hair, and sage vinegar can evaporate an overflowing toxic substance ivy or oak rash in a matter of moments.

Clary sage (Salvia sclarea) specifically is viewed as a lady's herb to a limited extent due to its estrogen-animating activity. The basic oil was first depicted to me by a companion, portraying how after the passing of her mom, she felt that a couple of drops of clary sage basic oil in the bath every night was the main thing that got her through. Normally, I expected this would be a strong, floral aroma with an establishing semi-sharp sage scent. My first sniff of clary was a serious stun, and it took me some time to build up an affection for it, however now I "get" it.

Clary sage fundamental oil's fragrance is thick, profound, and gritty. I can envision that it may give one the feeling of slithering into a protected, overgrown cavern. The plant itself is enormous with gigantic leaves that look somewhat like the customary nursery sages. The flower spikes are almost 12 inches (30.5 cm) of brilliant pinkish purple sprouts. Notwithstanding garden sage's properties of being germicide, antispasmodic, astringent, and antibacterial, clary sage is energizer, making it a fitting herb for PMS and different ladies' issues.

A portion of the more fancy salvias are enjoyable to develop and make scrumptious teas, yet don't appear to have the equivalent restorative characteristics or the rough lasting development of nursery sage.
Sage's profound, rich, gritty quality is unequaled for culinary employments. Have a go at setting a wise leaf around a shrimp before enclosing it by bacon and preparing. Pork and sage was, one after another, as acclaimed as savvy stuffing for Thanksgiving supper. Sage can help in the processing of fat, so it was remembered for greasy meat plans.

Restorative Benefits
- Reduces irritation
- Inhibits oxidation
- Enhances memory
- Kills organisms
- Treats sleek skin and hair

Sage Tea

This tea is ideal for a sore, scratchy throat or when a bug is getting you down. I truly prefer to utilize a licorice root stick as a stirrer for the additional relieving properties.

Ingredients

- 2 teaspoons dried savvy or 5 or 6 new leaves
- 1 cup (235 ml) boiling water
- Juice of 1/2 lemon
- Honey to taste

Yield: 1 cup (235 ml)

Instructions

Steep the sage in the boiling water for at any rate 5 minutes. Evacuate the savvy, include the lemon squeeze and honey, and drink.

Note:

You can make sage and lemon honey ahead, and simply add that to heated water. Much the same as making a vinegar or a tincture, hack the wise fine, cut the lemon dainty, and when you've filled the container 66% full with them, pour a decent quality nearby honey (crude is ideal) over them, utilizing a chopstick to ensure everything is all around covered. I keep that in the fridge until it is required. The honey is an incredible additive.

Hiker's Rash Relief

I utilize this throughout the entire summer on rashes from plants, bug nibbles, and the entirety of summer's skin tingles. It is modest and simple to make. You can skirt a herb or two in the event that you can't discover it, however don't avoid the sage! Use about a balance of herbs, with an overwhelming hand on the sage.

Ingredients

- Sage leaves (I use 'Berggarten' for its extremely high proportion of basic oil)
- Plantain leaves
- Yarrow flowers and leaves
- Jewelweed (cut from the get-go in the mid year when the stems are succulent and delicious)
- Apple juice vinegar

Yield: As wanted

Instructions

Join the herbs in a container and add apple juice vinegar to cover; permit to soak for a month if conceivable. Strain enough to fill a shower container and use. I leave the rest splashing for as long as could reasonably be expected.

Whole Sage Leaves

I opposed these for a considerable length of time, figuring they didn't sound generally excellent. What an immense error that was! Simply a year ago I chose to give it a go to use as an enhancement on some butternut squash soup, and it was difficult to limit myself from eating them all before the soup was even prepared.

Ingredients
- 2 tablespoons (28 g) unsalted spread
- Whole sage leaves

Yield: As wanted

Instructions
Dissolve the spread in a skillet and afterward slip the entire sage leaves in, warming until they get fresh, similar to rich, appetizing little chips of flavor ... where right? Gracious right. Channel on a paper towel. These will keep at room temperature for a few days on the off chance that they are in a hermetically sealed compartment.

Salvia Fritta

This is more muddled strategy for making seared sage leaves.

Ingredients

- 1 cup (226 g) coconut oil
- 1/4 cup (40 g) flour
- 1/4 cup (30 g) cornstarch
- 1/2 cup (120 ml) soft drink water
- 16 to 24 flawless sage leaves
- Sea salt

Yield: 16 to 24 sage leaves

Instructions

Warmth the oil in a griddle. While it warms, join the flour, cornstarch, and soft drink water in a bowl and whisk well.

Dig the savvy leaves in the hitter. At the point when the oil is acceptable and hot, include 4 or 5 of the leaves to the skillet, and fry until brilliant earthy colored. Channel on paper towels. Rehash until all the leaves are seared. I don't know to what extent these will keep. It's never occurred.

Spare the oil, this will be injected with sage flavor. You can utilize it to cook poultry, potatoes, or veggies later.

Sage Pesto

This formula utilizes garlic scapes, the empty cutting edges that develop in the spring only preceding a flower. The scapes must be sliced to forestall that sprout, keeping the vitality of the plant concentrated on the bulb of garlic under the ground. Scapes have gotten somewhat of a delicacy as of late, and are regularly found at ranchers' business sectors in the spring.

Ingredients
2/3 cup (160 g) olive oil, or more varying, separated
1 cup slashed garlic scapes
1 cup new savvy
1/4 cup (50 g) slashed pecans, toasted
1/4 cup (35 g) ground Parmesan cheddar

Yield: 3 cups (720 g)

Instructions
In blender, join 1/4 cup (80 ml) of the olive oil, the garlic scapes, and the sage. Mix on high.
While the ingredients are mixing, include the staying 1/4 cup (80 ml) olive oil in a stream. On the off chance that the blend is dry, include more oil. Include the nuts and mix quickly. Blend in the Parmesan cheddar by hand.

CHAPTER 4 - Making It Work For You

At the point when you walk the boulevards of any American city brimming with high rises, costly vehicles, TV satellites, and individuals stuck to flip telephones, it's difficult to accept that scarcely a century back most Americans lived near the land. Doubtlessly that progress has given us comforts and, in numerous occurrences, a simpler lifestyle. What it hasn't given us is a feeling of having a place. With each new innovation that protects us from nature and from the human network, we retreat more distant into our workplaces or lairs—and more distant from an extraordinary wellspring of solidarity and imperativeness.

The Native Americans comprehended their environmental factors more personally than we can envision. At the point when they took a gander at a tree or a field, they saw nourishment, medication, life. They watched their reality intently, scholarly its riddles, and found how to put it to the most ideal use.

America's medicinal services framework is among the best on the planet, and the clinical forward leaps we underestimate would have amazed the early Americans. In any case, this advancement has accompanied a cost. Prescriptions that battle illness with tiny accuracy regularly cause reactions that exacerbate us feel in different manners—and present day medication frequently treats our side effects, without animating the body's natural capacity to mend itself.

The facts demonstrate that Native Americans relied upon their healers much as we depend on our primary care physicians. They went to them for drugs and for direction in recuperation. Notwithstanding, they never dismissed the way that great wellbeing, similar to the wealth of nature, is an endless pattern of disclosure, confidence, and appreciation. Thus they watched life around them—and their wellbeing—intently. They learned. What's more, they offered gratitude for every single mending cure nature presented.

We, thus, can offer gratitude for the recuperating insider facts they have granted to us. There are such huge numbers of to browse! It doesn't make a difference whether you have low vitality, joint inflammation, or a terrible back—or on the off chance that you essentially scratched yourself early today in the kitchen. Several years prior the Native Americans had a considerable lot of similar issues and concerns, and the arrangements they found at that point are similarly compelling today.

In the accompanying pages you'll discover conversations of a considerable lot of the most well-known medical issues we face today, alongside the best Native American solutions for each condition. Make certain to talk with your PCP to preclude any genuine sickness before utilizing them, be that as it may. What's more, consistently utilize Native American recuperating methods to supplement—not to supplant—your primary care physician's consideration.

It's difficult to accept that common cures created and refined such a long time ago can supplement as well as now and then even outperform the capacities of present day medication. Be that as it may, it wouldn't have astonished the Native Americans. All things considered, they got their quality from Mother Nature, and there's no more noteworthy force for accomplishing great wellbeing.

CHAPTER 5 - Preparing Herbs

Local Americans' confidence in the recuperating intensity of herbs was risen to just by their creativity in utilizing them. They for the most part utilized all pieces of the plants, albeit various parts were set up in an assortment of ways. Herb utilize likewise shifted from clan to clan. Each healer had their own preferred plans and arrangements. Once in a while herbs were smoked through exceptional formal funnels, or consumed so the intense exhaust could be breathed in, or blended in with liquor as tinctures, or joined with creature fats to make ointments. Another, progressively crude, technique was essentially to bite a herb to discharge the oils, at that point apply it to the piece of the body where it was required. Some mending services called for patients to be ignited with the seething parts of specific herbs for the ideal restorative impact.

The most well-known herbal arrangements, in any case, weren't so fascinating. Truth be told, the shamans of hundreds of years prior arranged herbs similarly as botanists do today. You'll discover definite data on various methods for utilizing herbs in the books recorded in the list of sources. Yet, for fundamental use, here are the most widely recognized strategies:

Herbal teas: likewise called implantations, teas are made by soaking leaves, seeds, or bark in heated water. Natural teas are essentially utilized for drinking, in spite of the fact that the fluid might be applied remotely to treat cuts, consumes, hyper-extends, wounds, creepy crawly nibbles, or toxic substance ivy. To make a tea, put a teaspoonful of dried herb (or two teaspoons of new) in some boiling water and permit the blend to stand, or mix, for 10 to 15 minutes. This permits therapeutic mixes to liberate themselves from the herb and be discharged into the water. Strain the fluid utilizing cheesecloth or an espresso channel—or simply utilize a tea infuser—at that point drink when it's cool enough not to consume. Herbal teas lose their viability rapidly, so it's imperative to utilize them immediately. Following a couple of hours, a large portion of the recuperating force will be no more.

You can make more grounded teas by multiplying the measure of herb, yet that is commonly the cutoff. More than this sum won't make it increasingly powerful and may build the danger of symptoms.

Herbal decoctions: This technique is utilized for the woodier herbs, or when utilizing roots, stems, bark, seeds, or flowers from which the restorative mixes are not effectively discharged. Put an ounce of dried herb (or two ounces of new) in a 16 ounces of cool water in a pan. Heat the water to the point of boiling, at that point lessen the warmth and let it stew for 15 minutes to 60 minutes, contingent upon the herb. It's prepared to use in the wake of stressing the fluid and permitting it to cool. Similarly as with teas, decoctions are typically smashed as a tea, however they may likewise be utilized remotely as "washes" or bathwater added substances. At times they're utilized to drench a fabric for use as a pack.
Likewise with teas, decoctions are best just in the wake of blending. Be that as it may, they can be put away in a fixed holder in the cooler for as long as 24 hours.

Herbal poultices: Poultices are commonly utilized for outside issues, for example, wounds, injuries, skin aggravations, or growing, or for agonizing regions brought about by wounds, injuries, or joint inflammation. A poultice comprises of a "pound" that can be made by squashing new herbs to a glue consistency, or by boiling dry herbs for 10 to 15 minutes. Another, maybe less agreeable, choice is to do as Native

Americans much of the time chewed—the herb into a glue (without gulping) and afterward apply it to the skin.

Notwithstanding how a poultice is readied, it should be set in acceptable contact with the region being dealt with. This is typically done by applying the poultice legitimately to the skin, or by putting it between two bits of slim material, for example, bandage, which makes the method tidier.
A few people are delicate to specific herbs, and treated territories may blush or give different indications of disturbance. This may mean a hypersensitive response is happening, so you should stop the treatment right away.

CHAPTER 6 – Herbal Remedies And Your Child

In the event that you are keen on attempting any herbal cure with your youngster, it's critical to chat with your primary care physician first and counsel an accomplished botanist about use and dose. Similarly as with any drug, youngsters can react to herbs uniquely in contrast to grown-ups; so you should practice caution while directing any herbal treatment. The accompanying graph can be utilized together with sound clinical guidance to get ready herbal teas for babies, youngsters, and teenagers.

Suggested doses of herbal teas for children:

AGE	DOSE
0–1 year	$\frac{1}{20}$ of the adult dose
1–2 years	$\frac{1}{10}$ of the adult dose
3–4 years	$\frac{1}{5}$ of the adult dose
5–6 years	$\frac{3}{10}$ of the adult dose
7–8 years	$\frac{2}{5}$ of the adult dose
9–10 years	$\frac{1}{2}$ of the adult dose
11–12 years	$\frac{3}{5}$ of the adult dose
13–14 years	$\frac{4}{5}$ of the adult dose
15 and older	Full adult dose

CHAPTER 7 - Gathering Herbs

Local American cultivators got long stretches of preparing before setting out all alone, and they worked in a situation that was liberated from poisons, for example, bug sprays and substance manures—just as from neighborhood statutes. Current Americans, be that as it may, have more to battle with, says cultivator Ana Nez Heatherley. A couple of security insurances are basic.

Picking any plant, including therapeutic herbs, is illicit in certain regions, so be certain you realize the neighborhood laws before setting out.
Don't collect along occupied expressways or in different territories where there might be elevated levels of contamination.

Always be certain you know precisely what you're gathering. Picking and utilizing an inappropriate plant, Heatherley cautions, makes certain to accomplish more damage than anything else.
"Consistently think about the Earth and its prosperity before taking any plant," she says. Gather just from enormous gatherings of plants, and never take in excess of 33% of those that are accessible. Try not to take more than you intend to utilize, and harm the rest of the plants and encompassing vegetation as could reasonably be expected. As it were, treat the earth with a similar regard that Native Americans did.

Drying And Storing Herbs
Herbs are exceptionally transient in any event, when dry, and will rapidly lose their advantages except if they're appropriately arranged and put away.

Fresh herbs can lose intensity very quickly, so most cultivators dry them for capacity. To dry herbs, separate the leaves from the stems and spread them in free, single layers on a spotless, level surface. Bulkier plants might be dangled from a line in a dry zone, for example, a warm storm cellar or upper room. Flies and different bugs are now and then pulled in to herbs, so you might need to cover them with a layer of cheesecloth.

The time required for drying depends both on the herb and the earth in which it's being dried. Since herbs lose their strength so rapidly, the shorter the drying time frame the better. It for the most part takes about seven days. A herb is adequately dry when it despite everything has a smell yet is sufficiently dry to break. On the off chance that it disintegrates totally when you handle it, you dried it excessively long.

Roots, which ought to be completely washed before drying, take more time to dry than leaves and flowers—for the most part around three weeks.
When they are dried, store them in coated earthenware, dim glass, or metal holders with tight-fitting covers. Plastic packs or nourishment stockpiling holders will retain the fundamental oils.

CHAPTER 8 - Solutions For Common Ailments

Acne

An early Dutch pilgrim depicted the Native Americans as being "sound of body, all around took care of and without flaw." At when Europeans considered washing destructive and skin was not even close as solid as it is today, numerous onlookers wondered about the Native Americans' reasonable appearances.

Specialists presently realize that skin inflammation as a rule emits when oil organs in the skin become obstructed with cell flotsam and jetsam. At the point when the pores can't deplete, microorganisms may assemble inside, causing contamination and irritation. The best medications for skin inflammation are frequently the least difficult: great eating routine and cleanliness, alongside day by day washing and astringent items for evacuating oils and microscopic organisms.

It's farfetched that Native Americans stressed a lot over their skin—however at that point, they routinely did things that helped keep it solid and flaw free. Here are their privileged insights.

Sweat it clean. The Native Americans accumulated in sweat lodges for stylized ceremonies, yet the serious steam and warmth were useful for their skin also. Wet warmth opens pores in the skin, permitting them to deplete.

The most straightforward approach to make your own "sweat hold up" is to abound in the shower. With the washroom entryway shut, run the water as hot as you serenely can. To save vitality, a few people want to steam just their countenances. You can do this by warming a pot of water on the stove until it reaches boiling point. Expel from heat, at that point lean your face over the pot, hanging a towel over your head to trap the steam. Around 10 minutes of steam will open pores and help keep your skin sound. Try not to get excessively near the heated water or the pot, be that as it may, or you could be burnt.

Utilize a herbal scour. Washing your face in any event once per day with a decoction produced using mending herbs, for example, aloe, fennel, rose, savvy, watercress, or yarrow will open the pores and help scour away old oils. Simultaneously, herbal medicines help control the microbes that can prompt skin break out.

To clean particularly irksome spots, botanists suggest scouring the region with new, squashed garlic. Garlic is an amazing microscopic organisms contender and will help keep diseases from beginning. On account of garlic's impactful scent, the vast majority do garlic medications around evening time, allowing the skin to "let some circulation into" before morning.

Wash down your framework. The wellbeing of the skin straightforwardly mirrors the strength of the entire body. Local Americans often drank herbal teas, utilizing echinacea, dandelion, Oregon grape, stinging weed, or goldenseal. Taken as frequently as three times each day, these teas help to expel unsafe substances from the body's lymph framework while fortifying the purging forces of the liver and kidneys. They additionally reinforce the insusceptible framework, helping the body battle hurtful microscopic organisms.

Anxiety

Stress and uneasiness are a lifestyle for most Americans today, yet it wasn't constantly similar to this. Among the Native Americans, tension was uncommon, to some extent since they determined gigantic harmony and solace from their otherworldly convictions. As a seventeenth century student of history watched, "They have no claims and go to considerable lengths to gain the merchandise of this life, for which we Christians pain ourselves to such an extent."

Life wasn't ideal for Native Americans, obviously. During times of pain, starvation, or war, they encountered gigantic measures of pressure, similarly as individuals do today. The thing that matters is that they couldn't head to the drug store to fill a solution for the most recent tension relieving drug.
Luckily, they didn't have to, in light of the fact that they were knowledgeable in herbs that quiet the psyche and soul. Researchers today have discovered that herbs, for example, dandelion, valerian, bounces, dark cohosh, rose, and goldenseal, normally taken as a tea a few times each day, have normally quieting characteristics. In the event that time and comfort are factors, you can purchase these herbs as enhancements or tinctures in wellbeing nourishment stores.
Extraordinary compared to other mending herbs, flower petals, can be utilized remotely to soothe nervousness. Cultivator Ana Nez Heatherley suggests running a shower and adding new flower petals to the water. To finish the experience, you can entertain yourself by drinking some flower petal tea and perhaps hold a rose tea pack to your temple. Soon that is no joke once more.

Asthma

Asthma is almost at scourge extents, particularly among kids. Specialists gauge that in excess of 14 million Americans have asthma, a condition where aviation routes in the lungs become tightened and aggravated. Limited aviation routes cause wheezing and brevity of breath, and the aggravation brings about the creation of a lot of bodily fluid, which causes hacking and makes it much harder to relax.

As indicated by verifiable records, asthma seems to have been uncommon among Native Americans. Some portion of the explanation behind this is most likely ecological. Not at all like individuals today, Native Americans weren't presented to air contamination or swarmed day to day environments, the two of which can prompt asthma. Likewise, despite the fact that they smoked formally, they barely had the pack-a-day propensity that numerous Americans do.

Also, Native Americans routinely utilized herbs that are currently known to battle asthma. The different herbs act in various manners. Some are antispasmodics, which mean they help loosen up the bronchial fits that can trigger asthma assaults. Others are expectorants, which help expel mucus from the lungs. Still others are tranquilizers, which diminish the enthusiastic pressure that is a typical asthma "trigger."
Asthma can be a major issue, so it's fundamental to work with a specialist before attempting natural cures at home. When asthma is leveled out, it's fine to add herbal teas to the treatment.

Cultivators exhort assaulting asthma with herbs from every one of the three mending gatherings, utilizing the accompanying diagram.

ANTISPASMODICS	EXPECTORANTS	SEDATIVES
black haw	garlic	black haw
milkweed	milkweed	mullein
valerian	mullein	valerian
garlic	peppermint	hops
fennel	licorice	lady's slipper
licorice		
peppermint		

Back Pain

It's difficult to overemphasize the effect of back pain on Americans today. Specialists gauge that 80 percent of us will have back issues sooner or later in our lives, costing us in physical agony and enthusiastic anguish, yet in addition in billions of dollars of clinical and different expenses. Among Native Americans, in any case, back issues were generally uncommon. This proposes for all that we do that is off-base for our backs, they accomplished something right.

The Native Americans were truly dynamic, which implies that their back and muscular strength were solid. They were infrequently overweight and they encountered generally little everyday pressure, the two of which assume a job in keeping the back sound. In any event, when they got back pain, they knew precisely how to guarantee that it didn't deteriorate. You might need to attempt a couple of their mysteries.

Warmth it up. As fans of the perspiration stop, Native Americans consistently presented their backs to damp warmth. Clammy warmth warms muscles so they remain free and flexible. It additionally expands flow, which can flush pain causing metabolic results from the lower back. Most Americans don't have sweat lodges, obviously, however what we improve in light of the fact that it's progressively advantageous: a hot shower. Absorbing high temp water at home or thriving in a whirlpool shower at the fitness center will rapidly lessen back pain—and, all the more significantly, keep the muscles nimble so there's less danger of back wounds later on.

Get a back rub. Scouring the muscles accomplishes more than release them up. It additionally may flush out agony causing poisons, for example, lactic corrosive, which regularly add to back pain. As per student of history Virgil J. Vogel, among the Cherokee, "The medication man initially warmed his hands over live coals, at that point focused on the influenced section a roundabout movement with the correct hand, a large portion of the weight being applied with the palm."

We can exploit a similar strategy today. Back rub specialists are prepared to see how the muscles work and how to apply the proper strain to calm various types of agony. You can locate an affirmed knead specialist by glancing in the telephone directory—or approach your primary care physician for a suggestion.

Drink peppermint tea. Peppermint contains a compound called menthol, which has pain relieving and muscle-loosening up properties. The most effortless approach to take peppermint is as a tea, which you can drink as regularly varying to soothe pain.

Make a peppermint rub. Local Americans frequently scoured sore muscles with a liniment produced using peppermint. The menthol in the peppermint drummed up some excitement of warmth that entered profound into the muscles. To make a herbal rub, freely fill a container with new peppermint leaves, include enough vegetable or mineral oil to cover the leaves, top the container, and store it in a cool, dim spot, shaking it a few times each day. Following 10 days, strain off the oil and store it in a dull container. When back pain strikes, rub the oil altogether into the muscle for speedy help.

Or try sage. Like peppermint, sage can likewise be applied to the skin to help mitigate back agony. To make a savvy rub, blend a couple of drops of sage oil, accessible in wellbeing nourishment stores and herb shops, with a few tablespoons of vegetable oil. Dunk your fingers in the oil and apply it to your back as regularly varying.

Set willow to work. A famous pain executioner among Native Americans, willow works similarly just as headache medicine, yet is to some degree gentler on the stomach, particularly on the off chance that you make a tea that likewise incorporates licorice root.

Remain as dynamic as could be expected under the circumstances. Specialists gauge that 90 percent of back pain episodes could be maintained a strategic distance from in the event that we tried doing what the Native Americans did each day: work out. Exercise fortifies the muscles in the back and guts, which thus lessens the measure of day by day pressure on the spine.

Exercise doesn't need to be formal or even particularly thorough to be advantageous. Strolling is incredible exercise for forestalling back pain. So is planting. Walking here and there steps. Doing housework. For whatever length of time that you're truly dynamic, you'll normally fortify the muscles that are basic for ensuring the back.

Here are a couple of extra tips for diminishing and forestalling back pain:

Sitting is challenging for the back, so it's essential to get up and move around, regardless of whether it's only for a couple of moments once 60 minutes.

If you invest a great deal of energy sitting, set aside the effort to locate an excellent seat with great lumbar (lower back) support.

Keep your back straight however much as could reasonably be expected. Regardless of whether you're simply getting a sock from the floor, twist your knees instead of your back.

When lifting, attempt to keep your back and legs in arrangement. Turning the middle when lifting is extremely hard on the back.

Sleeping on solid bedding offers extra help for the lower back, which can help forestall issues later on.

Awful Breath

At the point when student of history John Lawson wrote in 1714 that the Native Americans he met around North Carolina were "among the best individuals on the planet," he wasn't simply discussing their attitudes. Alongside numerous different onlookers of the time, Lawson saw that, contrasted with Europeans, the Native Americans were out and out fragrant. In addition to the fact that they took visit showers, however their refreshing eating regimens, joined with great dental cleanliness, kept their breath new too.

Awful breath is typically brought about by microorganisms that collect on the teeth, tongue, and gums. The Native Americans every now and again utilized herbs that helped control microscopic organisms and furthermore had sweet, crisp smelling flavors. As indicated by herbal power James A. Duke, Ph.D., a portion of these cures worked better than the locally acquired items we use today.

Bite on fennel or cardamom. The seeds of the two herbs are charmingly fragrant and normally refresh the breath. What's more, they contain a microscopic organisms murdering compound called cineole, which keeps rank microbes from aggregating. Bite the seeds altogether and either swallow them or let out the shells once the flavor has been depleted.
Eat some parsley. This new, lush tasting herb is an incredible wellspring of chlorophyll, a similar fixing that is utilized in numerous breath mints, says Dr. Duke.

Wash with peppermint or sage. Both of these sweet-smelling herbs have antibacterial properties. The leaves are excessively solid to eat, however they're extraordinary for making tea for washing. You can rinse with the tea similarly as you would with a store bought mouthwash.

Constipation

Given what we presently think about the impacts of physical movement on remaining ordinary, it's far-fetched that stoppage was a typical issue among Native Americans. Be that as it may, they more likely than not had a few issues with stoppage since they developed the firstever instrument for giving bowel purges. It was a syringe-like gadget, with the empty leg bone of a fledgling toward one side and the bladder of a little creature or fish at the other. In spite of some innovative upgrades, bowel purges are given similarly today.

Another Native American treatment for obstruction was a biting gum produced using the tars of the amber tree. This treatment appeared well and good since biting gum is known to help loosen up the guts because of the expanded creation of salivation, which contains stomach related proteins and can go about as grease. They had numerous other herbal solutions for stoppage also, a couple of which are as yet utilized today.

Take herbal fiber. Specialists have discovered that dietary fiber is the best treatment for blockage since it ingests water in the internal organ. This makes stools bigger, which animates the digestive organs to move them along more rapidly and without any problem. Probably the best wellspring of fiber is seeds from the plantain plant. The psyllium assimilates colossal measures of water, making it probably the best cure you can discover.

To make a psyllium purgative, include a teaspoonful of plantain seeds to some boiling water, permit to cool, at that point drink, seeds and all, more than once per day. Make certain to drink a ton of water when utilizing psyllium since it expels a ton of water from the body.

A few people are touchy with the impacts of psyllium, notes natural power James A. Duke, Ph.D. On the off chance that psyllium makes you awkward, you can get comparative impacts by eating more high fiber nourishments, for example, entire grains, natural products, vegetables, and beans.

Another herb that is high in fiber is flaxseed. It doesn't break up in water the manner in which psyllium does, so instead of blending it in fluid, it's ideal to add it to nourishments, for example, oats or hand crafted breads. Take one to three tablespoons per day, and drink a lot of water, Dr. Duke exhorts.

Invigorate the digestion tracts. You would prefer not to utilize it time after time, yet rhubarb root is an incredible diuretic that animates the digestion tracts. To utilize rhubarb, puree three stalks in the blender, being certain to expel the leaves, which are dangerous. Include some squeezed apple, a teaspoonful of lemon juice, and a tablespoonful of honey, and drink it once per day. Be that as it may, notice: "Its diuretic activity can be really amazing," Dr. Duke cautions.

Coughs

At once, many hack drops contained licorice, a herb that alleviates the throat and helps go about as a hack suppressant. Local Americans were completely mindful of the forces of licorice. They regularly bit the root, despite the fact that at times they made licorice teas.

Other herbal teas that help diminish hacks incorporate mullein, stinging bramble, magnolia, sassafras, honeysuckle, red clover, and the bark from trees, for example, resin, pine, wild cherry, and birch. When making bark tea, you have to heat up the bark for 15 minutes to discharge the dynamic fixings.

Despite the fact that teas are powerful, an additionally mitigating procedure is to make a herbal syrup, which waits longer on aggravated tissues in the throat. Botanist Ana Nez Heatherley suggests the accompanying plans.

Red Clover Cough Syrup

Ingredients

- 1 ounce new (or one-half ounce dried) red clover flowers
- 1 cup high temp water
- 2 cups sugar

Place the ingredients in a pot and heat to the point of boiling. Diminish the warmth, stew for 10 to 15 minutes, at that point strain the fluid and empty it into a glass container with a tight-fitting top. Top quickly and store in a cool, dim spot or in the cooler. Accept one teaspoonful varying.

Mullein-Honeysuckle Cough Syrup

Ingredients

- 1 tablespoon new (or 1 teaspoon dried) honeysuckle flowers
- 1 tablespoon new (or 1 teaspoon dried) mullein leaves
- 2 cups honey

Place the ingredients in a pan and heat to the point of boiling. Lessen the warmth and stew gradually for 20 minutes. Strain the fluid and empty it into a container with a tight-fitting top. Store the syrup in a cool, dim spot or in the fridge. Accept one teaspoonful varying.

Depression

Students of history disclose to us that Native Americans were commonly a cheerful people, inspired by their confidence in the kindness of Mother Earth and every one of her manifestations, plants and creatures the same. This is the equivalent versatile soul that Native American psychotherapist Robert Blackwolf Jones attempts to ingrain in his patients when they're feeling down. "See Mother Earth," he lets them know. "Every one of her winged creatures sing. Every one of her trees influence. Every one of her waters sprinkle. She lives with the solid heartbeat of life."
We should all endeavor to live so happily, yet when it's essentially unrealistic, we can likewise hope to Mother Earth for help.

A few sorts of sadness are too genuine to even consider treating all alone. It's critical to chat with an advocate or doctor on the off chance that you are encountering bitterness that just won't leave, sentiments of sadness or uselessness, changes in eating or resting propensities, or self-destructive contemplations. More often than not, be that as it may, misery isn't this genuine, and a gentle instance of "the blues" can be lifted with nature's assistance.

The Native Americans accepted that keeping their bodies in top condition would normally light up the feelings too. With a blend of ordinary exercise, great sustenance, and the intermittent utilization of state of mind lifting herbs, they had the option to keep their spirits high in any event, when life brought them low. There are numerous herbs that can influence state of mind, however here are the most widely recognized and all around considered.

Licorice root. St. John's wort has been getting a ton of consideration of late as being "nature's Prozac," yet licorice, which was regularly utilized by Native Americans, is thought by numerous botanists to be similarly as significant. "No plant has more energizer mixes than licorice," as indicated by herbal position James A. Duke, Ph.D. "In any event eight licorice mixes are monoamine oxidase inhibitors, which are mixes fit for strong upper activity."
To get the advantages of licorice, drink up to three cups of licorice tea daily, prepared new or made by adding licorice tincture to some boiling water.

Caution: Licorice can have a harmful impact when taken for an all-encompassing timeframe, so you ought to think of it as a transient cure just—particularly on the off chance that you have hypertension or heart issues.

Purslane. "An incredible 16 percent of this herb comprises of energizer supplements when estimated on a dry-weight premise," says Dr. Duke. Purslane contains magnesium, potassium, calcium, folate, and lithium, all of which have upper impacts. The most ideal approach to utilize purslane is as a plate of mixed greens green.

Oats. As indicated by cultivator David Winston, oats are rich in the "nerve-sustaining" supplements calcium, magnesium, and B vitamins. Oats, he says, can "relieve the frayed sentiment of copying the light at the two closures." If you couldn't care less for oats, you can make an oat tea.

Scented herbs. Rosemary and sweet clover were utilized by Native Americans since they accepted their charming smells could help raise the spirits. Botanists prescribe balancing little

packages of these sweet-smelling aromatics around the house or
in your office.

Fever

A fever is frequently one of the main signs that you're becoming ill. It is anything but a charming inclination, which is the reason the vast majority do everything conceivable to bring down fevers as fast as could be expected under the circumstances. Getting your temperature down to 98.6 degrees will cause you to feel better immediately. Be that as it may, emotions can be misleading. At the point when you're wiped out and have a gentle fever, bringing down it is about the most noticeably terrible thing you can do.

Microscopic organisms and infections can just get by at specific temperatures. The fever you get when you're debilitated isn't a piece of the ailment; it's a piece of your body's safeguard. "By warming itself up, the body hinders the development of attacking creatures," clarifies John C. Roers, M.D., of the Department of Family Medicine at Baylor College of Medicine in Houston.
Native Americans comprehended the significance of fever. Not exclusively did they frequently let fevers run their course, some of the time they made things more sultry by sending hot individuals into sweat lodges. As it were, the perspiration stop was just a room-sized "fever."

Specialists today are probably not going to send patients with fevers into steam rooms. It isn't so much that they can't help contradicting the standard. It's simply that the vast majority wouldn't be eager to do it. So a tradeoff has been reached. Specialists as a rule prescribe letting a fever run its course as long as it's under 103 degrees. Higher temperatures, or any fever that endures longer than 48 hours, ought to be looked at by a specialist.

Be that as it may, to beat gentle contaminations and low fevers, it merits really trying to understand from Native Americans. They utilized herbs considered diaphoretics that raised the internal heat level only enough to give the resistant framework an additional lift. As per cultivator David Hoffmann, these herbs help "the bodies own innate recuperative forces."

Herbs that are suggested for fever incorporate cayenne, ginger, sage, peppermint, boneset, goldenseal, milkweed, Hops, rose, honeysuckle, and yarrow. These herbs are best taken as teas, which fills the twofold need of keeping the body hydrated while cleaning out the very germs they murder. Include a teaspoon of dried herb (two teaspoons assuming new) to some boiling water. Permit to soak for 15 minutes, strain, and drink up to three cups every day.
To bring down a fever, Native Americans utilized willow bark, which contains salicin, a fever-lessening compound like the dynamic fixing in ibuprofen. Simply steep a teaspoon or so in some boiling water for 15 minutes, strain, and drink varying.

Caution: Because willow bark contains mixes like those in ibuprofen, don't offer it to kids, as it might expand the danger of a conceivably genuine neurological issue called Reye's disorder.

CONCLUSION

We'll never know precisely what spurred the primary Native American, who arranged willow bark to bring down a fever, or how shamans found the wellbeing giving advantages of back rub, or what enlivened some valiant soul to thrash himself with nettle to assuage the agony of joint pain. What we cannot deny is that early Native Americans were profoundly pulled in to nature's puzzling powers and constantly examined their general surroundings.

They without a doubt saw that flying creatures, deer, and different creatures ate certain plants just when they were debilitated—and submitting their general direction to the brutes, they attempted these cures themselves. Different disclosures more likely than not been made by some coincidence: a tea alcoholic for enhance was found to ease sleep deprivation; smoky corn cobs in the fire appeared to quit tingling; and carefully seasoned new dandelion mended liver issues.

Native Americans didn't become master healers short-term. Each revelation, the triumphs alongside the disappointments, was passed along to succeeding ages. Despite the fact that they had little information on science or the natural functions of the body, hundreds of years of experimentation—what researchers today may call contextual analyses—gave them the information they expected to keep individuals sound.

Their inheritance lives on. A considerable lot of the cures utilized by Native Americans hundreds of years prior are despite everything utilized today, by their relatives, yet additionally by cultivators and doctors all through the world. In certain nations, actually, natural cures are utilized as much as or more than present day drugs. Why? Since nature's fixes have been demonstrated to be protected and successful, and they frequently cause less symptoms than present day drugs. Also, as any specialist will let you know, that is acceptable medication.